IN ACTION

Coaching for Extraordinary Results

THIRTEEN

CASE STUDIES

FROM THE

REAL WORLD

OF TRAINING

JACK J. PHILLIPS

SERIES EDITOR

DARELYN "DJ" MITSCH

EDITOR

ASTD

Linking People,
Learning & Performance

Ordering information: Books published by ASTD can be ordered by calling 800.628.2783 or 703.683.8100, or via the Website at www.astd.org.

Library of Congress Catalog Card Number: 2002105503

ISBN: 1-56286-322-3

Table of Contents

Introduction to the *In Action* Series

Like most professionals, the people involved in HRD are eager to see practical applications of models, techniques, theories, strategies, and issues relevant to their field. In recent years, practitioners have developed an intense desire to learn about firsthand experiences of organizations implementing HRD programs. To fill this critical void, the Publishing Review Committee of ASTD established the *In Action* casebook series. Covering a variety of topics in HRD, the series significantly adds to the current literature in the field.

The *In Action* series objectives are as follows:

- *To provide real-world examples of HRD program application and implementation.* Each case describes significant issues, events, actions, and activities. When possible, actual names of organizations and individuals are used. Where names are disguised, the events are factual.

- *To focus on challenging and difficult issues confronting the HRD field.* These cases explore areas where it is difficult to find information or where processes or techniques are not standardized or fully developed. Emerging issues critical to success also are explored.

- *To recognize the work of professionals in the HRD field by presenting best practices.* Each casebook represents the most effective examples available. Issue editors are experienced professionals, and topics are carefully selected to ensure that they represent important and timely issues. Cases are written by highly respected HRD practitioners, authors, researchers, and consultants. The authors focus on many high-profile organizations—names you will quickly recognize.

- *To serve as a self-teaching tool for people learning about the HRD field.* As a stand-alone reference, each volume is a practical learning tool that fully explores numerous topics and issues.

- *To present a medium for teaching groups about the practical aspects of HRD.* Each book is a useful supplement to general and specialized HRD textbooks and serves as a discussion guide to enhance learning in formal and informal settings.

These cases will challenge and motivate you. The new insights you gain will serve as an impetus for positive change in your organization. If you have a case that might serve the same purpose for other professionals, please contact me. New casebooks are being developed. If you have suggestions on ways to improve the *In Action* series, your input will be welcomed.

Jack J. Phillips
In Action Series Editor
P.O. Box 380637
Birmingham, AL 35238-0637
phone: 205.678.8038
fax: 205.678.0177
email: serieseditor@aol.com

Preface

Coaching is fast becoming the hottest topic in organizational and leadership development, but most organizations struggle to find the best approaches to employ the coaching concept in their organizations or to measure coaching's impact. There often is confusion about what constitutes effective coaching and how to define or gauge success.

Through this casebook we hope to contribute to the understanding and employment of coaching practices and ideals by offering a variety of approaches, processes, strategies, and models, while showing the wide range of opportunities for those who seek and work with coaches to go beyond what they thought possible. The authors, who reflect viewpoints from varied backgrounds, are pioneers who are shaping the profession and creating benchmarking processes for effectively coaching individuals, teams, and entire organizations.

Target Audience

This book should interest anyone involved in HRD or organizational development (OD), executive leadership, management, and coach training. The primary audience is organizational practitioners who are struggling to identify the most credible processes and resources for delivering coaching services and monitor their impact and who have requested more tangible examples of effectiveness. This same group also has expressed concern that there are too many models, methods, strategies, and theories, and too few examples of excellent results. This publication should satisfy practitioners' needs by providing both the studies and the stories of great results from coaching.

The second audience comprises coach instructors, professors, and business students. Whether this casebook is used in university classes with students who are pursuing coaching as a potential career or in helping to develop a critical skill or required competency for executives and managers, it will be a valuable reference. Many of the authors have shared proprietary models and offer seminars and adjunct sessions to further explore the concepts herein. The book also can be used to supplement a standard HRD or learning textbook or to complement a coaching textbook or coursework. As a supplemental text, this casebook will bring practical significance to the coursework, convincing students that there are systematic strategies, processes, methods, and models that can help to ensure the successful and consistent implementation of coaching skills as a practice for creating more effective communication and leadership influence. It will also inspire anyone who studies it to host dialogues about life-purpose and life-values and the impact of these conversations in the realm of global business.

A third audience is the managers and other leaders who are learning that coaching is the technology of professional development that accelerates energy, alignment, and performance because people are pulled toward goals rather than pushed toward them by company mandates. In organizations where speed and innovation are key ingredients for success, managers will consider coaching a primary tool.

Each audience should find the casebook entertaining and engaging reading. Questions are placed at the end of each case to stimulate additional thought and discussion. One of the most effective ways to maximize the usefulness of this book is through group discussions, using the questions to develop and dissect the issues, techniques, methodologies, and results.

The Cases

The most difficult part of developing this book was to enroll case authors to contribute their views, definitions, systems, processes, and models that would provide a strategic approach to coaching. In the search, electronic invitations were sent to more than 10,000 individuals who have expressed interest in coaching. To tap the global market, more than 2,000 of the individuals contacted were outside the United States. We selected 13 case studies for this publication. These cases present a variety of approaches and represent several industries, including manufacturing, telecommunications, networking, pharmaceuticals, and nonprofits.

In our search for cases, we contacted the most respected and well-known organizations in the world, leading experts in the field, key executives, and well-known authors and researchers. Although coaching is a relatively new profession, we believe these cases represent best practices. Many of the experts producing these cases characterize them as the best examples of coaching in the emerging profession. We do know that if these are not best practices, it will be difficult to find them in other publications.

Although some attempt was made to structure cases similarly, they are not identical in style and content. It is important for the reader to experience the studies as they were developed and to identify the issues pertinent to each particular setting and situation. The result is a variety of presentations with a variety of styles. Some cases are brief, outlining in concise terms what happened and what was achieved. Others provide more detailed background information, including details on how the people involved determined the need for the process, descriptions of the personalities involved, and explorations of the coaching engagement as a unique and precious partnership.

Because it is helpful to show a wide range of approaches, we made no attempt to restrict cases to a particular methodology, technique, or process. We resisted the temptation to pass judgment on various approaches, preferring to let the reader evaluate the different techniques and appropriateness in their particular settings. As are most other business development practices, coaching is subject to interpretation. We are aware there will be differences of opinion about some of the assumptions, methodologies, and strategies, and discussion about what method is most sound or comprehensive. We also are aware that these will vary depending on the reader and his or her specific application of the information. These cases are a gift from the authors, and each reader will determine their usefulness by employing, improving, or re-creating the ideas presented.

Case Authors

It would be difficult to find a more impressive group of contributors to a publication of this nature. Because coaching is a dynamic and relatively new professional field with emerging talent, we expected to publish the thought-leaders in the field and we were not disappointed. These creative, experienced, professional, and knowledgeable authors are on the leading edge of coaching. Most are professional or master certified coaches through the International Coach Federation. A few are published authors who already have made a tremendous contribution to the field and have taken the opportunity to provide an example of their top-quality work. Others have made their mark quietly and have achieved success for their world-class organizations. We attempted to provide cases from Japan, Europe, and Australia, where coaching is also an emerging technology, but because of the language constructs and the formats for this book, it was too difficult for those thought-leaders to share this time. We hope to produce another work that will showcase and compare some of the practices in other areas of the world.

Suggestions

As with any new publication, we welcome your input. If you have ideas or recommendations regarding presentation, case selection, or case quality, please send them to ASTD *In Action* Series Editor, Box 380637, Birmingham, AL 35238-0637; phone: 205.678.8038; email: serieseditor@aol.com. These comments will be not only appreciated but also acknowledged.

Acknowledgments

Although this casebook is a collective work of many individuals, the first acknowledgment goes to all of the brilliant professional coaches, HRD professionals, and the researcher who served as case authors. Getting the creative spirits in this group to follow a structured format or rewrite something so intuitive was a challenge. We are very grateful for their professional contribution, and for the energy invested in making this book a reality. We also want to acknowledge the organizations that have allowed us to use their names and cases for publication, specifically, Nortel and Verizon, which disclosed so much information about their internal practices. We realize this action is not without risk. We trust the final product has portrayed them as progressive organizations interested in results and willing to develop new processes and cultures as a result of coaching applications.

I also want to acknowledge Jack Phillips for introducing the concepts of action-oriented and bottom-line-focused solutions through the *In Action* series. His partner, Patti Phillips, has been my primary contact and has continued to create possibilities for what this work can mean in the world, as we prove that coaching works. I would also like to thank Joyce Alff, the editorial director, who gently nudges us to create a clear and substantial work. Joyce manages the *In Action* series writing process and keeps everyone on track, edits our work, and laughs with us (via email) when we have rewritten for the fifth time and are ready to just move on. Her willingness to contribute her insights, wisdom, and the time it takes to see a project through was a blessing. My company, The Pyramid Resource Group, also employed our internal project coordinator, Courtney Davis, to assist in composition. Courtney must also be acknowledged for her unflappable and courageous acts as a sounding board. She gave me feedback about my personal efforts that I trusted and included. She also acted as a lens through which we could view first draft compositions by newer authors and helped to craft directive memos for cases to be rewritten. She assisted us in many aspects of the book's composition, including producing tables and graphs.

As always, it was a joy to work with the staff at the American Society for Training & Development. The managers of book publishing are always supportive, professional, and very helpful. ASTD is again leading the way in this effort to measure effectiveness of a human development technology.

Quality publications are always a result of the efforts of many people, including the time spent by those who read these cases. If you have taken the time to read this book or if you purchased it to use as a textbook for yourself, a group, or an organization, then we would like to express our gratitude for your support. This is a groundbreaking casebook. Thank you for helping us create best practices from our work as coaches and for exploring the extraordinary results available through coaching!

Darelyn "DJ" Mitsch
Cary, NC
October 2002

How to Use this Casebook

The cases presented in this book illustrate a variety of coaching approaches for assessing or measuring results. Collectively, they offer a wide range of client cases, techniques, processes, and strategies. Moreover, they represent a wide spectrum of industries including pharmaceuticals, manufacturing, nonprofits, and telecommunications.

As a group, these cases represent a rich source of information about the strategies of some of the best coaches in this emerging field. Each case does not necessarily represent the ideal approach for any other specific situation because coaching is a dynamic and intuitive process, one that follows the client or company. In every case, it is possible to identify areas for improvement. That is part of the learning process and the intention of a casebook—to build on the work of generous thought-leaders who willingly share their experiences.

Table 1 provides an overview of the cases by industry, key features, and case coach. It can serve as a quick reference for readers who want to examine the cases by particular audiences, industries, and types of cases.

Using the Cases

There are several ways to use this book. Overall, it will be helpful to anyone interested in the topic of coaching, whether that person is a senior-level executive, an HRD/HR/OD professional, professional coach, professor, or student.

Beyond that, four specific uses are recommended:

1. Professionals can use this book as a basic reference for practical applications of coaching. A reader can analyze and dissect each of the cases to develop an understanding of the gaps addressed, the approaches, and, importantly, improvements or augmentations to the process.

2. This book will be useful for group discussions, during which interested individuals can react to the material, offer different perspectives, and draw conclusions about innovations and methodologies.

Table 1. Overview of case studies by industry, focus, and target participants.

Case	Industry	Focus	Target Participants for Coaching
Nortel Networks	Telecommunications	Measuring the value of coaching for Leadership Edge team	Nortel Leadership Edge candidates Top talent managers
Global Telecommunications Firm	Telecommunications	Coaching to increase leadership, align key responsibility areas, measure retention and productivity	Sales managers
Verizon Communications	Telecommunications	Coaching key executive during merger	Key executive
National Nonprofit Organization	Nonprofit	Coaching an executive to initiate changes in company culture	Nonprofit vice president reporting to board of directors
Grand Pharmaceuticals	Pharmaceuticals	Team coaching program	Sales team
Bob's Construction Company	Construction	Assisting client in balancing work and personal life	Company president
Trilogy Scientific	Scientific research and development	Coaching newly hired director to make transition from academia to corporate executive	Director of research and development
International Telecommunications Organization	Telecommunications	Developing a strategic cultural initiative	Management team—front line to executive level

Manufacturing Company	Manufacturing	Coaching to provide a confidential sounding board for a major company's CEO	Company CEO
KBY Financial Services	Financial institution	Coaching a star performer whose confidence was undermined by the challenges of a new position and an unsupportive boss	Newly appointed vice president of sales
Metropolitan Nonprofit	Nonprofit organization	Coaching to ease strain between the executive board and the CEO	Organization's CEO
Health-care Clinic	Health care	Coaching general manager for guidance in dealing with superiors, vendors, and staff, and to keep perspective in client's personal life	Clinic's general manager
Vision Telecom	Telecommunications	Assisting executive in developing a vision for the company's information technology and billing operations	Company executive

3. This book can serve as an excellent supplement to other books about coaching or management textbooks. It provides the extra dimension of real-life cases that showcase the often *extraordinary results* from coaching interventions.

4. This book will be extremely valuable for managers and executives who must expand their competencies and skill sets to include coaching as a method of developing people and improving succession planning. HRD/HR staff often support these managers, and it is helpful for them to understand the methodologies these professionals employ and the value of coaching as a cultural context for HR interventions.

Follow-Up

Space limitations have required that some cases be shorter than the author and editor would have liked, and some information concerning background, assumptions, strategies, and results had to be omitted. If additional information on a case is needed or desired, please contact the lead author of the case or the editor. In most instances the address of the lead author is provided in the biographical information offered by each person at the end of his or her case; the address of the editor is provided in the preface and in the biographical information at the end of the book.

Coaching for Extraordinary Results

Darelyn "DJ" Mitsch

Organizations throughout the world are finding ways to integrate professional coaches and systemic approaches to coaching as ways to create desired changes in company culture. The applications of coaching are as varied as the providers and the companies who employ them. Implementing coaching as a consistent process has raised many questions, including how to define coaching competencies and expectations; how to distinguish coaching from consulting, training, and therapy; and how to determine the bottom-line impact or return-on-investment (ROI). In answer to these questions, this book includes a host of great coaching stories that embody the concepts and principles of organizational coaching.

When a coach is employed as a true partner, growth always occurs beyond ordinary performances and accomplishments. Quite often there is evidence of an extraordinary outcome, an alignment of values, and even a hint of magic in the results experienced by those coached and those they influence. The cases presented here are both the "study" of what happened as well as the "story" of what happened through the coaching process and partnership.

Coaching is a method of personal and professional development that at the core is primarily about conscious inquiry and learning. Many have turned this simple view of an important human need— for people to live meaningful lives and engage in significant, fulfilling work—into lengthy and eloquent definitions suitable for hanging on a paneled office wall. We try to make this need for fulfillment, one so organic to human nature, into something objective enough to duplicate and measure as a technology. We do this because we work in a world in which our minds have become trusted above the heart and intuition. We inquire, "So what if coaching has opened a leader to a new view of his values in his work as the CEO of a manufacturing company? What does it matter that he works in alignment with values of service and beauty?" The answer is that through his discoveries in coaching conversations, he created a global company strategy to have a zero impact on environments his company once polluted and re-created the company to set a new course of leading the world in "green" standards. How do you measure this or any other profound leadership legacy in a formula?

Starting in the early 1990s, coaching became a new business and personal development term used by a handful of consultants, retired sports coaches-cum-authors, motivational speakers, financial advisors, therapists, and corporate refugees. There was a realization that people learn in different ways and that emotions drive behavior. There was also a great opportunity for many leaders to better manage professional development for their staffs and teams. Schools and programs were launched to fill the need for coaching skill development. Corporations launched programs to call their supervisors and managers "coaches." Since then, coaching has been deemed a cost-effective way to offer customized leadership development, craft new career directions, and address performance concerns. Coaching has helped people gain language for self-expression—to "get real" in their workplaces, to expand the views of mandated goals for alignment with core values, and to gain perspective.

A Model for Extraordinary Coaching

A model for extraordinary coaching could take many forms, but the one that seemed common to these cases is illustrated in figure 1.

Step One: Client Engages Coach

In the first step of the coaching model, the coach and client begin an engagement prompted by any number of people. The client can be an individual executive, a professional, a team of people, or a company. Examples in this book include

- a manager hiring a coach for development of a talented key player
- a CEO hiring a coach for personal and professional growth
- a new vice president seeking to find her "groove" with a newly inherited team and engaging a coach through HR)
- a coach offering a series of free sessions to a client
- a senior executive seeking an internal HR executive to coach him through a merger.

Figure 1. Stages of developmental coaching for executives or companies.

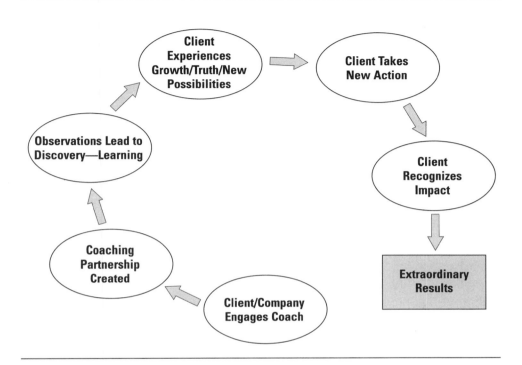

Executive coaching is one of the primary points of entry for all organizational coaching. Either an internal corporate coach or an external professional coach who partners with an executive or a group of executives will open the opportunity for further coaching in the organization. Many of the stories in this casebook describe the result of executive coaching initiatives. The International Coach Federation (ICF), the nonprofit professional society of coaches throughout the world, sponsors the annual Executive Summit, a conference of many prominent executive coaches. A white paper posted on the ICF Website (www.coachfederation.org), which was presented as a result of Executive Summit I, defines executive coaching in the following way:

> Executive Coaching is a facilitative one-to-one, mutually designed relationship between a professional coach and a key contributor who has a powerful position in the organization. This relationship occurs in areas of business, government, not-for-profit, and educational

organizations where there are multiple stakeholders and organizational sponsorship for the coach or coaching group. The coaching is contracted for the benefit of a client who is accountable for highly complex decisions with wide scope of impact on the organization and industry as a whole. The focus of the coaching is usually focused on organizational performance or development, but may also have a personal component as well. The results produced from this relationship are observable and measurable, commensurate with the requirements the organization has for the performance of the person being coached.

Another point of entry for coaching in organizations is through a connection with the HR department or organizational development (OD) team. These professionals often have a mandate for leadership development and look to coaches to provide specific services to bolster key training objectives for developing core competencies in managers, either individuals or specific groups in which there is a focus on leadership development. For example, leaders are expected to be proficient in budgeting, projecting profit and loss, ensuring quality processes, and managing operational processes. OD professionals will often employ contract consultants, trainers, or universities to help create foundation programs for these core competencies or defined company expectations. Needs often surface during these processes for these executives to become seasoned leaders of the teams they manage. For example, the focus might be to influence, mentor, and retain key talent. Once these needs are identified as a point of entry for coaching, the HR or OD professional will seek to hire a qualified coach for the individual or the group.

Step Two: Coaching Partnership Created

The coach and client form a partnership based on open communication, intimacy, and trust. The coach is responsible for setting the stage, understanding the client's agenda, and clarifying expectations. The coach is not concerned with building a long-term friendship but in having the courage to explore untapped areas and challenging the client to take full ownership of desired outcomes. Because the focus is always on the client's agenda, the coach often will establish a nonreporting relationship with the company that puts the client in charge of expressing the value or impact of coaching. For this reason, and because many results are qualitative and self-reported, there have been few measures of the impact of coaching. On the following pages we have cases that describe the qualitative and sometimes intangible impact as well as the quantitative ROI results.

Step Three: Observations Lead to Discovery and Learning

The contract or agreement in this partnership between client and coach is that the coach will serve as a guide to the client's inner wisdom, truth, and best answers. The coach only advises where she or he has the expertise, exploring other areas by asking powerful and sometimes "naïve" or "stupid" questions. This "quest" allows the client to become an observer, gaining perspective and new views of possibilities through the coach's eyes. When people become introspective and begin taking full ownership of their lives and actions, then—and perhaps only then—discovery, expansion, and re-creation begin. People become more aware of the impact of their decisions and through this awareness they learn to make better decisions.

Step Four: Client Experiences Truth, Growth, and New Possibilities

People are happiest, most fulfilled, and most productive when they take actions that are aligned with who they really are and what they most desire to do. They will accomplish much more with less effort when they move in rhythm with their passions, natural talents, and commitments. Because companies are so dynamic and changes occur daily, learning to tell the truth versus playing a political guessing game leads to growth and the exploration of new possibilities. Coaching prompts truth telling, even if it is difficult, so that clients can see a host of new opportunities or actions to take. It is the power of these choices that opens the path for better decisions and more productive actions.

Step Five: Client Takes New Action

Clients create new ways to accomplish the extraordinary through coaching partnerships. They often do this outside the normal or expected timeframes because they are compelled rather than pushed to take better and more meaningful actions. Awareness is the key to adult learning; when aware, people cannot fall back into old patterns of behavior without some "yuck in the gut." Coaches hold clients accountable to themselves for taking best actions.

Step Six: Client Recognizes Impact

New actions provide new and often extraordinary results. Whether it's a measurable ROI for a developmental coaching engagement with an executive or an executive's visible determination to leave a meaningful legacy, coaching can accelerate a defined outcome and expected bottom line.

Step Seven: Extraordinary Results

In every case study written for this book, the results are extraordinary. Some can be calculated and defined. Others will resonate with the like-minded (or like-souled) and inspire both coaches and clients to have the courage for bolder actions and decisions. Some will prompt great discussions for future coaching initiatives.

The cases submitted for this book come from some of the world's most accomplished coaches. Some are recognized authors. Some are business executives and corporate refugees who have taken courses in coaching and bring many years of leadership experience to their work as professional coaches. Some work internally in large organizations to source leadership and coaching programs. All are the best possible authors for this first casebook on coaching and have been generous with their perspectives, stories, and processes. Each case is a gift to encourage coaches, executives, students, and OD professionals to continue defining a coaching path for extraordinary results.

The 13 cases featured on the following pages all have a stated and significant impact. In one breakthrough case, the company made a financial investment to develop key talent; in another, the company encouraged a group of employees to stretch toward a big goal. There are several stories that showcase individuals who achieved something extraordinary as a result of new perspectives gained through coaching. The bottom-line results from these cases cover a wide spectrum, ranging from the manufacturing CEO who changed a global company's strategy to have a zero impact on environments his company once polluted to the sales team that moved up three ranks in just four months.

Finding a Coach

Those who want resources to help find a coach or coaching company can refer to the following sources:

- This book's contributing coaches or authors can be reached easily through the biographical and contact information that follows each case study.
- The International Coach Federation's Coach Referral Service lists coaches by background, competencies, expertise, and focus area, so key words entered on the group's Website can produce a match.

Summary

In this casebook you will find great definitions for coaching that share a common theme: conscious learning and courageous actions that yield new results. The relationship described in all of the casework involves an individual client, a team, or the people of a large company partnering with a professional coach who provides perspective and explores the discoveries made in simple conversations. It is these discoveries and observations that lead clients to take new and better actions and, in turn, to produce better results. These results always translate to more meaningful work, higher productivity, the right people in the right jobs, people who are challenged to do their best, a leadership legacy, and a positive effect on the bottom line.

It is the need for learning and growth that intrigues professionals in the fields of human development and has companies of all sizes searching for the best approach to integrate coaching. By some reports, the business of training and development generates more than $70 billion annually, and self-help books about personal or professional growth are still the most popular bestsellers on nonfiction book lists. As a relatively new part of this training and self-help industry, coaching is not yet being measured to the degree of other business initiatives. However, coaching has been effective because it addresses the individual's specific needs for development, growth, and learning, which has a ripple-like effect in communication around and through the one being coached.

All of these emerging coaching applications address the needs people have to talk about their values, gain clarity about their futures, enjoy their lives, more gracefully manage the effects of mergers and other organizational changes in order to re-energize themselves and others, or to have some control in environments that seem out of control because of sped-up organizational changes. As success stories spread about people growing within organizations or accomplishing extraordinary results through coaching, the coaches who have been their guides are hired to create programs for other leaders and key talent. At some point, those who pay the bills pose the pivotal question: "How do we know this works?" The cases that follow answer this question.

The Return-on-Investment of Executive Coaching

Nortel Networks

Merrill C. Anderson, Cindy Dauss, and Barry F. Mitsch

Nortel Network's Leadership Edge program is focused on developing future leaders for the company. Coaching was a key component of Leadership Edge from the start, and informal testimonials of clients who had been coached had been very positive. However, once the coaches had completed the first engagement for Leadership Edge, the company asked, "How successful is coaching in delivering real value to the business and how can coaching be better leveraged in the future?" A groundbreaking study applied proven measurement methodology to document the financial and intangible value of coaching. This study provides critical insights into how coaching creates value in an organization and includes ideas on how to maximize the business value of coaching.

Organizational Profile

Nortel Networks is a multinational telecommunications company that operates in more than 150 countries. With more than 40,000 employees worldwide, the company specializes in providing communications technology and infrastructure for Internet, voice, and multimedia services. Nortel controls close to 90 percent of the North American broadband market, with close to 75 percent of all Internet traffic riding its optical network. The company also has leading market positions in wireless technology.

This case was prepared to serve as a basis for discussion rather than to illustrate either effective or ineffective administrative and management practices.

Background and Strategy

Nortel Networks is committed to developing its leadership capability in order to meet the demands of the challenging telecommunications industry. Leadership Edge was created to accelerate the development of next-generation leaders. Participants in the program are selected and sponsored by their business units based on their performance and the leadership potential they have demonstrated. They come from diverse global functions, including sales, marketing, technology, human resources, and finance, and represent a range of professional levels, from individual contributor to midlevel manager.

The development strategy for Leadership Edge involves formal assessments, including 360-degree feedback and personalized development planning in which coaching is a key component. Nortel Networks contracted with the Pyramid Resource Group (PRG) to provide coaching and coaching support services for the Leadership Edge program. PRG specializes in corporate coaching and provides a staff of certified coaches with extensive business backgrounds. Coaching gives participants the opportunity and the freedom to work privately with professional coaches who are skilled at helping individuals increase their overall effectiveness and leadership competency. Because the coaches come from outside the organization, participants are more willing to share their challenges and concerns without fear of potential consequences.

The coaching process began with a live orientation program. Potential coaching clients were also electronically provided with information to introduce coaching and establish expectations. Following orientation, a coach matching process was conducted by PRG, with input from Leadership Edge managers. PRG reviewed available assessment documents for each coaching client, conducted phone interviews with the clients, and then selected the most appropriate match from its team of senior coaches.

The coaching engagements lasted for five months, with two hours of telephone coaching each month. Coaches were available for email and phone check-ins as needed by their clients. During the program, coaches provided reports to PRG's project coordinator on the progress of each engagement and any trends they were observing with their clients. A comprehensive trends report was submitted to Nortel every three months to help the company assess progress. The information in the trends report was consolidated so coach/client confidentiality was protected.

Following completion of each coaching engagement, Nortel conducted a level one evaluation of the process. Qualitative feedback was gathered by the Leadership Edge coordinator, which was used to report back to the Nortel managers who were overseeing the overall Leadership Edge program.

Although participants spoke highly of their experience with coaching, Nortel Networks and PRG determined that a formal assessment of the business impact of coaching would facilitate future decision making when choosing among developmental alternatives. Therefore, they commissioned MetrixGlobal to conduct this study with the intention of understanding the following:

- how coaching added value for Nortel Networks, including the financial impact of coaching
- how Nortel Networks could best leverage coaching in the future.

Figure 1 shows the process that was used to analyze return-on-investment (ROI) for the coaching.

Figure 1. The process used to analyze ROI for the coaching.

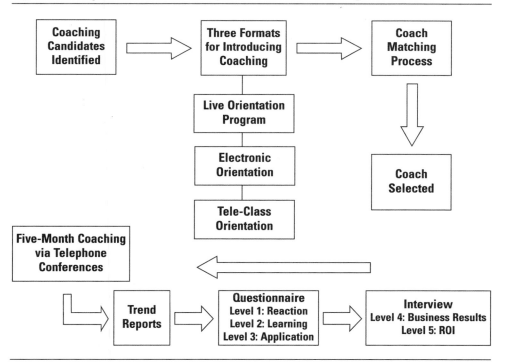

The Coaching Study
Data Collection Procedures

A questionnaire and follow-up interview were used to isolate and capture the effects of coaching on the business. Delivered electronically, the questionnaire examined participants' initial reactions to coaching, what they had learned, and how they had applied what they had learned. It also captured an initial assessment of business impact. The follow-up phone interview probed the potential financial ROI. This approach provided a consistent method of exploring the unique nature of each client's experience with coaching and how this experience translated into business benefits.

This study focused on six levels of data analysis (Kirkpatrick, 1977; Phillips, 1997):

- *Level One:* initial reaction of the clients to their coaching. The more positive the clients' initial reaction to coaching, the higher the likelihood that they will later experience valuable learning.
- *Level Two:* what clients learned from coaching. This demonstrates the extent to which the clients have gained the knowledge and insights they need to make meaningful enhancements to their performance.
- *Level Three:* how clients applied what they learned. The more frequently and effectively clients apply what they have learned, the greater the likelihood of their having a positive impact on the business.
- *Level Four:* the business impact of coaching. This shows how the changes that the clients have made created value for the business.
- *Level Five:* return-on-investment. It is important to know not only the total financial benefits of coaching, but also how this total compares to the total program cost.
- *Intangible Benefits:* Not all benefits can be documented in financial terms. However, because such intangible benefits as customer satisfaction are valuable to the business they are noteworthy.

Profile of the Respondents

Forty-three Leadership Edge participants were surveyed for the MetrixGlobal study; 30 responded, for a response rate of 70 percent. Most respondents reported having leadership responsibilities in such roles as people management, project management, and team leadership. Functional responsibilities included sales, finance, marketing, technology, and human resources. More than one-third of the respondents (37 percent) had direct customer contact as part of their job responsibilities, and 43 percent had direct reports. All but four were based in the United States. The average tenure with the company was six years, and 11 (37 percent) of the respondents were female.

Not all Leadership Edge participants received coaching. For the most part, coaching was provided to those people who requested it, but a few coaching respondents reported feeling pressure to participate. The study reinforced the need to provide a more formal introduction to coaching and ensure that participants understood the voluntary nature of the offering.

Measuring Impact

The results of the coaching study are described below, along with detailed discussion of the findings from each of the six evaluation levels.

Level One: Initial Reaction of the Clients to Their Coaching

As figure 2 shows, one-third (33 percent) of the respondents were initially skeptical that coaching would make a difference for them. Many of these respondents reported that they did not initially understand what coaching was or how it was going to help them. These issues, however, were not significant given the high ratings that both clients and coaches gave the initial two or three coaching sessions. According to 90 percent of the clients, these initial sessions provided a strong foundation for the coaching as objectives were set (90 percent reported favorably) and rapport was established (97 percent).

Figure 2. Level one: Reaction of clients.

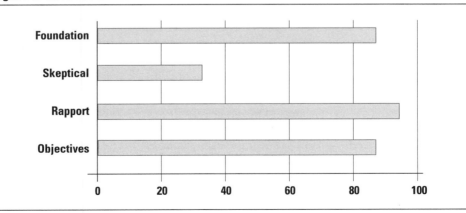

Level Two: What Clients Learned from Coaching

Figure 3 shows that almost all respondents (97 percent) gained critical insights into personal changes that they needed to make in order to be more effective. For 93 percent of them, this included realizing how to improve communication and collaboration skills. Eighty-three percent cited a better understanding of how to work with peers to accomplish business objectives. Gaining greater understanding of their personal impact on others (77 percent) and finding new ways to look at business situations (77 percent) were also cited as valuable. Overall, almost three-quarters (73 percent) of the clients learned how to be more effective as leaders.

Coaching sessions were characterized by the clients as rich learning conversations that fostered self-examination. Having the coaches come from outside the company was considered a benefit: Clients appreciated the relative safety of the coaching relationship, in which they could privately explore how to handle business situations. Many clients said that the coaching had enabled them to more rapidly develop as leaders and, in some cases, to develop differently as leaders. As a result of coaching, leadership styles were reported to be more inclusive of other's needs, less defensive, more supportive, and more focused on top priorities. Many clients reported being more careful in approaching situations and problems, more open to new ideas and alternative solutions, and—for those with customer contact—more effective with customer interactions.

Figure 3. Level two: Learning.

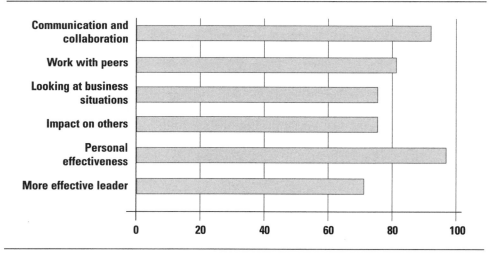

Level Three: How Clients Applied What They Learned

As figure 4 shows, seven of 10 clients were better able to handle real-life business situations as a result of the coaching they had received. Given the unique nature of each coaching relationship, the particular business situations that had been addressed would vary from client to client, but most (70 percent) were able to apply what they had learned during coaching to positively influence a business situation. More than half of the clients (53 percent) were better able to motivate others to accomplish business objectives. At least four out of 10 clients (47 percent) improved the quality or speed of decision making and were more effective working on business projects (43 percent). More than one-quarter of the clients applied their learning from coaching to improve team performance (30 percent) and to better utilize people and money (27 percent), and 13 percent reported increased retention of team members.

Additional applications for coaching included engaging others more effectively, dealing with restructuring, defining objectives and creating action plans to achieve these objectives, and better managing work/life balance.

Level Four: The Business Impact of Coaching

Three-quarters (77 percent) of the respondents indicated that coaching had significant or very significant impact on at least one

Figure 4. Level three: Application.

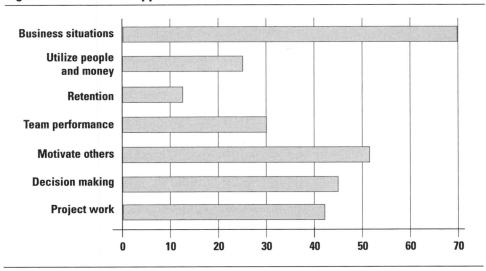

of nine business impact areas that were measured as a part of the study. During in-depth discussions conducted by telephone, more than half (60 percent) of the respondents were able to identify specific financial benefits from coaching. Figure 5 presents the nine business impact areas and shows the percentage of respondents who cited each as significantly affected by coaching. The figure also shows the percentage of respondents who cited financial benefits and the total financial benefits for each business impact area. The comments section provided additional information about the benefits documented by the participants.

Overall, participants cited personal or work group productivity and employee satisfaction as most significantly affected by coaching. More than $250,000 in documented annualized productivity benefits were recorded. Employee satisfaction could not be quantified but represented a significant intangible benefit to the company. As a result of the coaching, the participants were more satisfied and better able to increase the work satisfaction of their team members.

Work output and work quality were also cited by respondents as significantly affected by coaching: Nearly $1 million in increased work output for themselves and their work teams was documented. Because many respondents reported improvements in work quality but were not able to quantify these in terms of financial benefits, work quality improvements were considered an intangible benefit of the coaching.

The customer satisfaction and sales volume increases cited as influenced by coaching translated into increased net revenue; fixed cost reductions were documented by one respondent. Reductions in product cycle time were not identified as a benefit in this particular study, as no respondents were involved in activities that would affect this measure.

Figure 6 shows the five major sources of financial benefit gained from the coaching. Financial benefits gained from improvements in work output constituted 42 percent of the total financial benefit. Retention was the next greatest source of financial benefit, with 29 percent of the total. Increased sales contributed 14 percent of the total, productivity gains contributed 12 percent, and cost reductions contributed 3 percent.

Level Five: Return-on-Investment

- *Identifying business impact.* Calculations for determining the company's ROI in coaching followed the ROI process developed by Jack

Figure 5. Summary of financial impact.

Business Impact Area	Percent Citing Significant Impact	Percent Identifying Financial Benefit	Comments
Work Output	30%	20%	Benefits generated as a result of higher output of self or team through enhanced decision-making, collaboration, and accelerated achievement of objectives.
Work Quality	40	0	It was not possible to quantify these benefits and so, although substantial, these benefits will be considered intangible.
Productivity	60	50	Personal or team efficiency benefits expressed in terms of hours saved per week. Assumptions included $75 per hour, 48 weeks a year.
Cost Control	3	3	Reduction in sales and general and administrative expenses.
Product Development Cycle Time	10	0	Few respondents were involved in managing product development.
Employee Retention	27	13	Four team members said that they would have left Nortel Networks without the coaching. Three other team members said that coaching significantly influenced their staying with Nortel, but these three were not included in the benefits calculation. Two respondents mentioned retaining team members. These benefits also were not included.
Employee Satisfaction	53	0	This benefit was the second-most cited of all benefit categories; however, it was not possible to quantify this benefit in financial terms. This is another significant source of intangible benefits.
Customer Satisfaction	33	0	Most respondents who had customer contact indicated that customer satisfaction likely increased as a result of their changed behavior (due to coaching). This benefit was not directly measured and is considered an intangible benefit.
Sales Volume	10	10	Benefits are margin contributions to Nortel Networks (not total sales increases), based on 25% margins.
Total Financial Benefits			Financial benefits are not total benefits, but rather isolated benefits due to coaching.

Figure 6. Source of financial benefits.

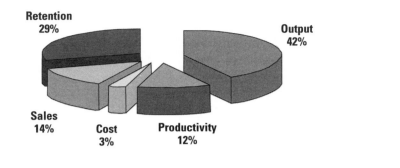

Phillips (1997). Following completion of the written survey, the researcher met with each respondent to document the financial benefits of coaching. Each discussion lasted about 20 minutes and focused on areas in which respondents indicated that coaching had a "significant impact" or a "very significant impact" on a key business area. With those who cited tangible financial benefits from coaching, the researcher probed to establish clear links between coaching and the client behaving in a different way and how this new behavior affected one or more of the business measurement areas. Forty percent of the respondents cited intangible benefits from the coaching but found it difficult to articulate tangible financial benefits. These intangible benefits could not be considered in the final ROI calculation.

- *Isolating the effects of coaching.* Each respondent was asked to estimate the percentage of the benefits attributable to coaching in order to isolate coaching from other factors that could have contributed to the financial benefits. These estimates ranged from 25 percent to 100 percent, averaging 75 percent. Respondents were then asked to estimate their level of confidence in their estimates, which in turn ranged from 30 percent to 100 percent and averaged 69 percent. The financial benefit identified for each respondent was then multiplied by both of these percentage estimates. Therefore, the financial benefits reported in this study are not the total benefits identified by the respondents but rather the benefits that were isolated as due to coaching.

For example, one respondent reported gains in personal productivity measured in terms of hours saved per week. She provided several examples of how, due to coaching, she was able to conduct meetings more efficiently and focus on higher priority work. She estimated a minimum of three to five hours saved per week, 80 percent of which was attributable to coaching. She was 75 percent confident in her estimate, so the benefits were calculated as follows:

3 hours @ \$75 = \$225 per week × 48 weeks = \$10,800 per year

This value was then multiplied by 80 percent (coaching) and 75 percent (confidence) to yield a financial benefit of \$6,480.

• *Determining the ROI.* Total program costs were tabulated by Nortel Networks and the Pyramid Resource Group. Costs included the professional fees of the coaches, evaluation costs, time the clients spent being coached, time spent to administer the coaching program and other administrative expense, travel, materials preparation, and all other expenses associated with the coaching program. It should be noted that although the costs of the entire program for 43 clients were included, the benefits were captured from only 30 survey respondents. In other words, the financial benefits from the 30 respondents were spread across the costs generated by 43 coaching clients.

Coaching produced an ROI of 788 percent for Nortel Networks. This was calculated by the following formula (Phillips, 1997):

ROI = [(\$ Benefits − Program Costs) / Program Costs] × 100

Summary of Intangible Benefits

Although they did not produce tangible financial returns, many benefits cited in this study did create meaningful value for Nortel Networks. For example, significant improvements were made in both employee and customer satisfaction, decision making was improved, and interpersonal relationships and collaboration were enhanced. The coaches reported that their clients developed skills in sizing up situations and more effectively motivating people and leading teams. Almost two-thirds (63 percent) of the respondents reported that coaching accelerated their personal development, improved team performance, and helped them to deal with organizational change. These benefits, although intangible, no doubt contributed in a positive way to the business.

Three-quarters (77 percent) of the respondents thought highly enough of their coaching experiences to recommend coaching to others at Nortel Networks. Those who recommended coaching stressed that, in order to get the most out of coaching, it was important to be open to self-analysis, to look at situations differently, and to try new approaches to address problems. Those who would not recommend coaching complained that the process was too open-ended rather than goal-oriented and that no answers were given by the coaches. Coaching was seen by this group as effective only in dealing with specific situations.

Lessons Learned

The following practices were identified as requirements for the most effective coaching intervention. Many were employed by PRG as a part of Nortel Network's coaching process; some were learned during the process.

- *Manage the entire coaching process to ensure consistency and quality.* Although the content of individual coaching sessions should always be confidential, the coaching process itself needs to be managed by the client company as well as the coaching company to ensure that the coaching clients and the coaches are following a meaningful process and leveraging client wisdom and best practices. It is critical to have a strong internal contact who works as a partner with the coaching company.
- *Prepare clients in advance for coaching and allow it to be a choice.* Because coaching remains a relatively new development technique, people may not understand how it can help them become better business professionals. The sooner they understand the process, the sooner they will see results. All potential participants need to attend an orientation session prior to beginning a coaching relationship to really understand the choices they have in the coaching process.
- *Offer clients the ability to select their coaches.* Chemistry is important to an effective coaching relationship. Provide prospective coaching clients with information about the coaches, including biographies, education, coaching credentials, functional expertise, industry experience, and other background information. Although the coaching company may offer a "best-fit" suggestion, there should be selection options.
- *Provide strong organizational support for coaching.* Those being coached should receive encouragement and support from their immediate managers. Also, coaching is most effective when conducted in the context of such developmental efforts as competency development, assessments, mentoring, and leadership workshops.

- *Ensure that coaches are introduced to the company's business and culture.* Coaches are more effective when they can identify with and talk about the realities of their client's environment. Although great coaching is an intuitive process, some background information makes for a fast start.
- *Allow each coaching relationship to follow its own path.* A major difference between coaching and training is that coaching allows the individual to determine what works best for him or her at a personal level. Coaches need wide latitude to work with "the whole person" and help each client become more effective as a person. This supports them in becoming more effective as business leaders.
- *Build performance measurement into the coaching process.* Evaluation of coaching is most reliable when designed into the process from the beginning to better set performance expectations and open up new opportunities to make coaching more effective while it is being conducted. For example, coaching can be refocused to deal with specific problems or to ensure that business priorities will be met. In this way, the evaluation becomes more than just a measuring stick—it becomes a structured approach to deepen the business rationale for coaching.

Questions for Discussion

1. How can you better position coaching with your client or your client's sponsor?
2. What strategies can you use to manage your client's expectations for the financial and intangible value of coaching?
3. How do you link the outcomes of coaching to your client's business objectives?
4. How can integrating measurement with coaching improve the results of coaching?
5. What concerns do you have about entering into conversations with your client about the financial ROI of coaching?

The Authors

Merrill C. Anderson is a business consulting executive, author, and educator with 20 years' experience in improving the performance of people and organizations. He is currently the chief executive officer of MetrixGlobal, a consulting company that provides clients with performance measurement solutions, and a clinical professor in education at Drake University. Anderson earned his doctorate at New

York University, his master's degree at the University of Toronto, and his bachelor's degree at the University of Colorado. He can be contacted at merrilland@metrixglobal.net.

Cindy Dauss has been with Nortel Networks since 1980 and has held both management and senior professional positions in a number of diverse areas, including marketing, training and development, human resources, and operations. Dauss was responsible for designing and managing Nortel's Leadership Edge program for the eastern United States and was instrumental in introducing coaching as a key component of the initiative. She has an undergraduate degree from Virginia Tech and a master's in business administration from Duke University's Fuqua School of Business.

Barry F. Mitsch is vice president of the Pyramid Resource Group. He has been involved in training and development activities for nearly 20 years, and his background includes work in both technical and non-technical training. Mitsch has designed and delivered classroom, self-instructional, and distance learning programs and specializes in group and individual presentation skills training for technical professionals. He can be reached at barry@pyramidresource.com.

References

Kirkpatrick, D.L. (1977). "Evaluating Training Programs: Evidence vs. Proof." *Training & Development,* volume 31, pp. 9-12.

Phillips, Jack J. (1997). *Return on Investment in Training and Development Programs.* Boston: Butterworth-Heinemann.

Coaching Makes an Unexpected Difference

Global Telecommunications Firm

Madeleine Homan, Linda Miller, and Scott Blanchard

A business unit of a global telecommunications firm engaged Coaching.com to provide a series of coaching sessions for 67 of its employees. The participants in the coaching process included all sales managers from the executive level to district sales managers. This intervention began early in 2001 and concluded for most participants in May 2001. It was the express intention of the coaching intervention to deliver results against the following key business objectives:

- *demonstrated increase in leadership capability*
- *improved alignment to achieve key responsibility areas*
- *measurable increase in the areas of retention, productivity, and value sales versus commodity sales.*

A third-party study performed three months after the coaching revealed that the coaching intervention had produced significant business and economic impact, specifically in the areas of improved retention, improvement in work environment, increase in productivity and revenues, and a decrease in the erosion of the customer base.

Organizational Profile

The client organization was a field sales division within a significant business unit of a global telecommunications company. Operating in more than 65 countries, the company offers Internet, voice, and data solutions that make business more productive, secure, and cost-effective. As measured by revenues and traffic carried, this organization is the leading global data, Internet, and network services provider. It generated revenues of $22.8 billion in 2001. Based on all forms of traffic, the organization carries more data over its networks than any competitor.

The field sales division, which was the client group, had had four successful years providing one percent of the company's overall revenues but four percent of its profits. The field sales division's era of hockey stick growth was slowing down, and it needed to move from an entrepreneurial environment to a mature process-oriented environment without losing passion and energy. The organization had 600 employees, 38 district sales managers, 11 regional sales managers, eight sales directors, five sales operations managers, and a vice president of sales.

Background

The training professionals who invited Coaching.com to discuss their business needs originally found out about Coaching.com on the Internet and expanded their research through conversations with the director of coaching services. A meeting between the client organization's two training directors and Coaching.com staff revealed a potential fit of service to business need. The vice president and senior leader of the client organization attended the meeting, and there was consensus that the organization did not need more training. (The organization had already invested significantly in Situational Leadership II, a key product of Coaching.com's parent company, The Ken Blanchard Companies.) Instead, the organization was interested in something fresh that would allow individuals to get what they needed to move forward. There was a great deal of synergy between the two companies, particularly since both actively use telephone and Internet technology to ease communication. This commonality immeasurably increased understanding and the impression of "fit." Once the business needs were understood, Coach.com proposed a combined solution that included consulting services and coaching services. Figure 1 presents a map of the events that carried out the proposed strategy.

Project Design and Implementation
Scope of Work and Objectives

The client organization agreed to use Coaching.com to do the following:
- develop key responsibility areas (KRAs) and impact maps for 11 of the client organization's positions. Impact mapping is a process that

Figure 1. Map of coaching events.

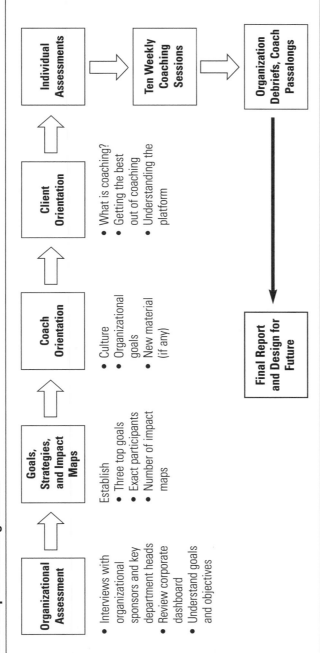

begins with identifying organizational goals, and then identifies and defines the strategic competencies by job role that are critical to the achievement of those goals.

- provide orientation to, practice with, and application of the standard Situational Leadership II (SLII) One-on-One Forms with individual coaching clients.
- help individual clients to emerge from their final coaching sessions with a completed professional development plan around their interviewing and recruiting practices, and with completed impact maps based on their KRAs.
- increase usage and application of SLII with coaching clients, based on individual coaching.
- provide general business coaching services to improve quality management practices and leadership skills and behaviors. A series of 10 coaching sessions (two sessions lasting up to one hour; subsequent sessions lasting up to 45 minutes) was provided to each manager over a four-month period.

Coaching.com agreed to provide consulting services (development of KRAs and impact maps for 11 positions, customized for the client organization) and project management services as needed. Coaching.com also agreed to provide the following individual coaching services:

- conducting individual coaching services with the client organization managers to achieve improved quality and quantity of one-on-one meetings with their direct reports
- assisting the client organization's managers with the completion of their individual impact maps, with the express purpose of aligning individual development plans, KRAs, unit goals, and business goals
- facilitating the completion and documentation of personal development plans, including, but not limited to, more effective use of SLII skills, utilization of effective hiring and selection practices, and improved frequency and quality of one-on-one meetings
- during sessions one and two, provide an orientation to the coaching process and the platform, with the first session to include management history and experience, assessment of SLII training, review of current important issues pending for the individual, and discussions regarding goals for the coaching experience
- during sessions three through 10, complete the self-assessment used on the Coaching.com Website. This trademarked Scrubdown process requires the client to decide that something is either true or not true, on the premise that clients will work on and be willing to change things about which they are currently telling the truth. Sessions three

through 10 also included a review of the KRAs and impact maps, application of SLII practices, review and practice with the one-on-one process, and completion of the impact maps and individual development plans.

Finally, Coaching.com agreed to generate reports to track the project:

- Monthly administrative reports reviewed important aspects of the coaching sessions from the data collected every week. The following trend data had to be reported by one third or more clients to ensure anonymity and confidentiality:
  — qualitative written data describing the themes that had emerged during coaching sessions, which had resulted in shifts of perspectives or attitudes
  — qualitative written data regarding the client organization's processes and policies that were or were not working
  — qualitative written data regarding the discrepancies between the client organization's leaders' actions and words
  — quantitative data regarding the number of sessions coaching clients had completed or missed, and if any clients had dropped out
- Project summary reports included an overall review based on the data presented in monthly reports.

The Coaching Process
Clients

Prior to their first sessions, the clients participated in an orientation designed to explain the following:

- what coaching is and is not
- why their company was investing in coaching
- what they could expect of their coaches and their coaching experiences
- what was expected of them
- the level of confidentiality they could expect
- logistical aspects involved in scheduling, using the Coaching.com Internet platform, cancellations, and coach/client mismatches.

During this orientation, participants heard about some early wins that their leader had experienced with his own coaching, which had started earlier by design. After the orientation, they used their log-on names and the passwords they had received with their Coaching Guidebook to navigate the Internet to the Coaching.com platform to take their Scrubdowns. They then used the automatic scheduler to set their first sessions with their coaches.

Once the clients were off to a good start with their coaches they could choose to use a prep form on the Internet platform to focus themselves and prepare their coaches for their upcoming sessions.

Coaches

Coaching.com coaches used the same basic process with each client. Prior to the first session with the client, the coach used the Scrubdown Calculator, a tool that uses information from the client to identify potential issues and focus areas. If there were focus areas that were unfamiliar to the coach, he or she could read up on the subject from the materials on the Website.

During their sessions with their clients, coaches did the following:
- established relationships with clients, assessing style and approach
- reviewed basic "housekeeping" details as needed
- debriefed Scrubdown experiences and reviewed responses
- discussed potential areas of focus for work together
- assessed "brushfire" areas that could be causing too much distraction and needed to be handled immediately
- connected to larger strategic focus areas where applicable
- discussed and clarified the confluence or opposition of personal goals with corporate objectives
- reviewed the impact maps and assessed areas for development.

At the end of each session the coach would ask a variation of the following to make sure that value was perceived:
- What will you take away from this session?
- What do you know, see, feel, or realize now that you hadn't before our session?
- What will you do differently moving forward?
- Is there anything you need to say to feel grounded, clear, and purposeful?

Over the course of later sessions the coaches continued to drill down into focus areas, setting clear SMART (specific, meaningful, attainable, relevant, trackable) goals, brainstorming and deciding on action steps, and reviewing activities for effectiveness. Accountability was offered according to client need as appropriate.

Measurement and Evaluation of Coaching Program

The following is an excerpt from the "Impact Evaluation Report on the Coaching.com Intervention." The study and report were designed and completed by Triad (2040 Raybrook SE, Suite 207, Grand Rapids, MI 49546; www.triadperform.com).

It was the expressed intention of the coaching intervention to deliver results against key business goals. The purpose of this impact evaluation was to determine if those results were produced, why and by whom, and if not, why not.

Background and Methodology of Study

The investigators used a "success case" methodology that sought to answer these questions:

- What business impact has this coaching intervention produced?
- What is the economic value of that impact to the client organization?
- When coaching produces a business impact, what contributes to that outcome?
- When participants do not see a business impact from their participation, why not?
- What can the client organization do differently or better to increase the impact of similar interventions that might be offered in the future?

The "success case" methodology uses a two-step approach to gathering impact data.

- *Step One.* An impact map was created for each job role to determine how coaching participants could use the coaching process to produce business impact. A survey based on that map was intentionally structured to help identify participants who claimed the most success in using the coaching process to produce positive business impacts.

The survey was emailed to 59 coaching participants. Fifty participants returned completed surveys, for a return rate of 95 percent. Figure 2 presents the survey, and figure 3 shows the results.

After completed surveys were returned, the investigators strategically selected individuals for in-depth interviews. For "success cases," the selection criteria included the following respondents:

— those who selected either "high" or "very high" when asked to rate the business impact of the coaching intervention

— those who were equally distributed by region of the country, by job role, and gender.

"Low success cases" were selected using the demographic criteria. On the question of overall positive impact from the course, these individuals rated the business impact of the coaching intervention as "low." The investigators interviewed each of only three of 55 respondents who selected this response.

Figure 2. Coaching initiative-impact survey.

Directions: Select your response to each question by clicking on the radio button for your answer. When finished, click on the Submit button. Your responses will be treated confidentially. Thank you!

1. When I began participating in the coaching sessions, I had very clear goals for my participation.

☐ Strongly Disagree   ☐ Disagree   ☐ Agree   ☐ Strongly Agree

2. The coaching sessions helped me better understand what I needed to change/do differently if I was going to help achieve our business goals of increasing employee productivity, protecting current pricing, retaining the best employees, deeper account penetration, etc.

☐ Strongly Disagree   ☐ Disagree   ☐ Agree   ☐ Strongly Agree

3. My coaching sessions gave me the skill and confidence I needed to do things that were important to achieving my own and my company's goals.

☐ Strongly Disagree   ☐ Disagree   ☐ Agree   ☐ Strongly Agree

4. I have learned some things about effective coaching from this process that I am already using with my direct reports.

☐ Strongly Disagree   ☐ Disagree   ☐ Agree   ☐ Strongly Agree

5. My manager was extremely supportive of my participation in this coaching process.

☐ Strongly Disagree   ☐ Disagree   ☐ Agree   ☐ Strongly Agree

6. Overall, the impact that the coaching sessions have had on my own and my company's business goals has been:

☐ Very Low   ☐ Low   ☐ Somewhat   ☐ High   ☐ Very High

- *Step Two.* Using the role-specific impact maps as guides, in-depth interviews were conducted with survey respondents who had reported either high or low impact from the coaching. These interviews took between 20 and 40 minutes. In some cases, investigators received permission to talk with direct reports and managers of those interviewed to corroborate the stories they had shared.

  Using all of the data from the surveys and the nine "success case" and three "low success case" interviews, the investigators arrived at the key findings and recommendations that follow. These are supported by multiple data sources, including all survey and in-depth interview data; they are never based on comments or data from a single source or only a few sources.

Figure 3. Results of the coaching initiative-impact survey.

Q.1 When I began participating in the coaching sessions, I had very clear goals for my participation.

Choice	Count	Percentage Answered
1. Strongly Disagree	1	1.8%
2. Disagree	17	30.9%
3. Agree	29	52.7%
4. Strongly Agree	8	14.5%

Q.2 The coaching sessions helped me better understand what I needed to change/do differently if I was going to help achieve our business goals of increasing productivity, protecting current pricing, retaining the best employees, deeper account penetration, etc.

Choice	Count	Percentage Answered
1. Strongly Disagree	2	3.6%
2. Disagree	5	9.1%
3. Agree	29	52.7%
4. Strongly Agree	19	34.5%

Q.3 My coaching sessions gave me the skill and confidence I needed to do things that were important to achieving my own and my company's goals.

Choice	Count	Percentage Answered
1. Strongly Disagree	0	0.0%
2. Disagree	3	5.5%
3. Agree	33	60.0%
4. Strongly Agree	19	34.5%

Q.4 I have learned some things about effective coaching from this process that I am already using with my direct reports.

Choice	Count	Percentage Answered
1. Strongly Disagree	2	3.6%
2. Disagree	2	3.6%
3. Agree	23	41.8%
4. Strongly Agree	28	50.9%

Q.5 My manager was extremely supportive of my participation in this coaching process.

Choice	Count	Percentage Answered
1. Strongly Disagree	2	3.6%
2. Disagree	2	3.6%
3. Agree	22	40.0%
4. Strongly Agree	29	52.7%

Q.6 Overall, the impact of the coaching sessions on my own and my company's business goals has been:

Choice	Count	Percentage Answered
1. Very Low	0	0.0%
2. Low	3	5.5%
3. Somewhat	11	20.0%
4. High	29	52.7%
5. Very High	12	21.8%

Key Findings

- *The Coaching.com intervention produced significant business and economic impact.* Both the survey data and the in-depth interviews provided ample evidence that this intervention produced, and will continue to produce, significant impact. Specifically, the investigators found abundant evidence that this intervention contributed directly to these KRAs:
  — Top-performing staff had been retained.
  — A positive work environment had been created.
  — Revenue had been increased by moving formerly average performers to a point at which they were exceeding their plans. A revenue increase may be too much to expect, given the company's year-to-date revenue levels. However, this conclusion is not about the company's revenue but about the way in which the coaching intervention helped managers work more effectively with targeted individuals. The accurate question would be: "How much farther below plan might the company have been if the coaching initiative had not been in place?"
  — Reduced erosion in customer-based revenues and customer satisfaction occurred due to the ability to fully staff territories more quickly when vacancies occur. Figure 4 gives a breakdown of the economic impact of coaching.
- *The intervention will have long-lasting impact on the client organization's people and business.* Fully 92 percent of all survey respondents indicated that they had learned coaching techniques they are now using with their direct reports; figure 5 shows the results. Thus the impact has had a cascading effect in the organization. A coaching approach is a very powerful way to develop a highly accountable, empowered workforce that is quick to respond to opportunities that provide high levels of customer satisfaction. A consulting approach is typically driven from the top and is slow and not very responsive to customers. In this intervention, participants experienced the power of the coaching process and found themselves receiving great benefits. It proved so beneficial that participants are willing to use the process with their reports. The long-term impact will be significant.
- *There was confusion on the part of participants about whether they were working with a coach or a consultant.* At the beginning of the process, many participants wanted the Coaching.com coach to tell them what to do in response to a specific need. Initially, the refusal of the coaches to do this frustrated some participants, but

Figure 4. Economic impact of coaching.

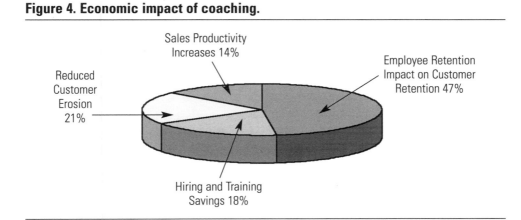

Sales Productivity Increases 14%

Employee Retention Impact on Customer Retention 47%

Reduced Customer Erosion 21%

Hiring and Training Savings 18%

Figure 5. Percentage of respondents who benefited from coaching.

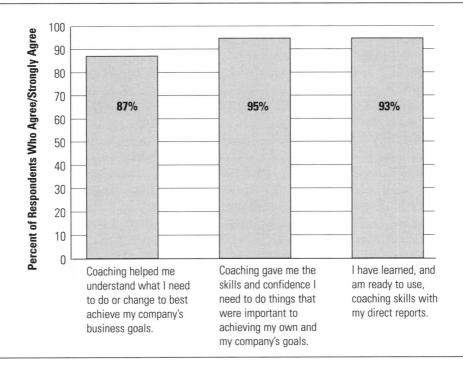

87%	95%	93%

Percent of Respondents Who Agree/Strongly Agree

Coaching helped me understand what I need to do or change to best achieve my company's business goals.

Coaching gave me the skills and confidence I need to do things that were important to achieving my own and my company's goals.

I have learned, and am ready to use, coaching skills with my direct reports.

most discovered that the coaching process was about their discovery of solutions. They appreciated that the coaches stuck with the coaching approach because they felt as if they ended up owning the actions and were excited to see how they played out.

- *The process did not have a clear exit strategy.* Many participants were uncertain about the next steps, if any, that would follow their 10 coaching sessions. Most participants suggested that they would like to have had an account of three to five more coaching sessions that they could schedule as needed over the next six to 12 months. Managers suggested that it would be helpful if they could have an "account" of 20 to 40 coaching sessions that they could make available to their direct reports on an as-needed basis. These messages meant that participants found great value in this process and wanted to have more sessions available, but to be used as they determined.

- *Participants wanted more control over the scheduling of their sessions.* A significant number of participants thought they needed to have a coaching session each week for 10 weeks. After the third or fourth session, many would have liked to schedule their next sessions based on need or have more time to take the actions they had planned in their most recent sessions.

- *Sponsorship of this initiative at the executive level of leadership in the organization made the business impact more likely.* The level of engagement of senior leaders in this coaching process was highly effective, contributing significantly to its success. Individuals talked about how engaged their leaders had been in this process and how often they had been asked about progress and how it was helping the business. These messages from management made the coaching intervention visible, important, and worth investing with time and energy. This also led to a significant level of internal discussion among participants about their coaching experiences and the process. This further reinforced the value of the intervention.

- *The timing of this intervention contributed to the high level of business impact.* The coaching intervention taking place during a time of changing organizational structure, reporting relationships, and sales processes increased the business impact. The client organization's staff members asked very hard questions about their commitment to the client organization; whether they would fit into the new structure, roles, and processes; and what level of anger they should direct toward the organization if they felt the changes were unfair or inappropriate. Having a third-party coach available during this time helped many individuals work through the above issues and, in fact, helped them move through the organizational changes with greater commitment to the client organization, to their work, and to their managers and direct reports. Specifically, participants said they were able to discuss some of these tough issues with their managers, some of whom effectively coached direct reports who were considering leaving the client organization. Quite a few participants found their personal commitment to the client organization changed for the better.

- *Participant openness to the coaching process made a decided difference in the personal and business impact that was achieved.* Those who reported the highest levels of personal and business impact were excited by the coaching opportunity. In fact, a number of those interviewed indicated that they had considered engaging a personal coach or mentor before this coaching initiative was announced. They perceived the client organization's commitment to this process as very positive and could not wait to get started.

   The three out of 55 respondents who reported little business impact perceived the process as a time for them to meet with a "shrink" because they were not performing well and needed help. These individuals were unable to take full advantage of the coaching process.

- *Significant business and personal alignment among individuals and within teams occurred as a result of the coaching intervention.* Individuals frequently reported that they used their coaches to help them solve less-than-ideal working relationships with their managers or with one or more of their direct reports. Many commented that the use of the impact maps, especially with their direct reports, brought significant alignment on critical business issues. Others indicated that they found themselves talking and working with their managers much more effectively. In these cases, their coaches had helped them develop approaches and strategies to bring about the desired change. In one situation, a manager used his coach's support to help two employees whose competitiveness was causing their team to function poorly. Both are now working effectively together and exceeding their individual plans.

- *This intervention demonstrates how people and performance can be positively changed using a process and not an event.* When a performance improvement intervention is spread over time and built into the doing of the job—as this intervention was—very positive results can be expected. Had this been one intensive 10-hour experience, the impact would have been only a small fraction of what was produced.

The coaching process allowed participants to work on new behaviors over time, create shifts in perspective that otherwise might not have occurred in the classroom in two days, and integrate their coaching into their jobs, rather than just learning about coaching. The client organization and Coaching.com used a very powerful process that produced significant business value.

- *A neutral third-party coach proved valuable at several levels.* Participants in this intervention described how they had talked with their coaches about issues that they had difficulty raising with their managers or direct reports, ending up with plans, strategies, and options for raising those difficult issues.

When third-party coaches begin working in organizations, there is often a concern that this process might drive a wedge between persons being coached and their managers. This evaluation proved quite the opposite. Instead of separating the manager and direct report, it served to bring them together, helping them to become aligned with key business goals and bringing about more effective working relationships.

The third-party coach also provided a safe haven in which to try ideas and approaches, build confidence, create strategies for raising concerns and problems, and bring about clarity and support among staff. Because the coach was not connected to the client organization, the participants were confident that there was no underlying agenda on the coach's part. They saw their time with their coaches as a "free discussion zone." However, it should be noted that coaches did not allow "gripe" or "victim" sessions, but focused on personal accountability and action.

Closing Thoughts

The vision of Coaching.com is to democratize coaching in organizations, using the best that all technologies have to offer. After years of working with individuals, the company suspected that the impact of coaching on individuals would improve the bottom line if coaching was delivered on a large scale in organizations. Now there is proof.

Although it wasn't relevant to coaching objectives, the client organization went through a reduction in force and reorganization in the middle of the coaching initiative. The anecdotal evidence that coaching provided much needed relief for those undergoing inordinate stress is abundant. One evening the sponsor called and used the term "divine intervention" about the serendipitous fact that 14 Coaching.com coaches happened to be serving in his organization at a time of such intense change. The experience for us as coaches and tireless advocates for coaching was profoundly moving.

Questions for Discussion

1. If you had a chance to re-create the coaching initiative outlined—with the objectives—what would you change in the original design?
2. How were the sudden reduction in force and reorganization factors in the success of the coaching?
3. In your estimation, was the assessment of economic impact fair?
4. How might the economic impact have been measured differently?
5. What was it about the coaching that made such an impact?

The Authors

Madeleine Homan, chief coaching officer and founder of Coaching.com, was the head coach on this project. With more than 12 years of coaching experience, Homan was an original advisory board member and senior trainer at Coach University and recently served as the vice president for professional development for the International Coach Federation, of which she is a founding board member and from which she earned the master certified coach designation. She has designed and led several coaching programs for international organizations, including PictureTel, Credit Suisse, and Forrester Research. She was the head coach and program manager for a coaching initiative at a New York investment bank, which rolled out coaching to support a new competency-based performance system to 2,100 employees worldwide. Homan's responsibilities at Coaching.com include design of coaching initiatives; coaching content and process development; and oversight of staffing and training, and the development of coaches. She can be reached at Madeleineh@coaching.com.

Linda Miller is vice president of coaching services at Coaching.com and was the senior coach on this project. After her introduction to coaching in 1995, Miller has focused on the launch and expansion of coaching within the corporate arena. In 1997, Corporate Coach U hired Miller to serve as director of training, where she was responsible for overseeing 200 certified coaches and for all on-site training. Since joining the Coaching.com team in 2000, Miller has been responsible for the development of coaching infrastructure, the deployment of coaches, and overseeing all implementation of major client initiatives. Miller has coached and trained corporate leaders and their teams, including Allied Signal, Boeing, Deloitte and Touche, Delta Faucet, Duke Energy, and US West. Miller is a founding recipient of the master certified coach designation from the International Coach Federation and is a member of the National Speakers Association.

Scott Blanchard is CEO and founder of Coaching.com and was the lead consultant for this project. Blanchard serves as a director of the Ken Blanchard Companies. He is an experienced business consultant, trainer, and speaker. Prior to the creation of Coaching.com, he helped manage large training initiatives in the financial services, automotive, software, telecommunications, retail, and service industries. Scott holds a master's degree in organization development from American University.

The Internal Executive Coach: Coaching Through a Merger

Verizon Communications

Nancy K. Philabaum

The merger of GTE and Bell Atlantic formed Verizon, the world's largest provider of wireless and wireline communications in the United States, as well as the largest directory publisher in the world. The merger brought with it many changes within the executive ranks, where—as often happens in such situations—senior positions were occupied by executives whose backgrounds and experience were not directly related to the functions they suddenly found themselves leading. The intervention of a coach in these situations can often smooth the transition for the executive. This case study explores the ways in which the company's internal executive coach partnered with one such executive, the newly appointed executive vice president of HR, to meet the challenges of his new position and help establish the foundation for his leadership team.

Organizational Profile

With more than 132 million access-line equivalents, Verizon is one of the world's leading providers of communications services. A *Fortune* 10 company with operating revenues in 2001 of more than $67 billion, it has a domestic footprint spanning the coasts. Verizon also has a presence in 40 nations and boasts 247,000 employees. The telecommunications giant offers local and long distance service, as well as advanced communications products and services, both wireline and wireless. Leading a function in a company of this magnitude is an awesome responsibility.

This case was prepared to serve as a basis for discussion rather than to illustrate either effective or ineffective administrative and management practices.

The merger of GTE (100,000 employees) and Bell Atlantic (160,000 employees) was one of the largest mergers in history. Many resources were required to successfully make the transition from two cultures to one Verizon, and coaching played a unique and fulfilling role in this transition. Because the scale of change was magnified in this context, the influence of coaching was likewise magnified. This is exciting for the coach and efficient for the organization. Coaching executives through a merger of this magnitude was a tremendous honor.

Background

More than 70 percent of the senior executives from GTE chose to leave the merged entity within the first year. This situation left GTE employees wondering about their fates, and if the decision-making focus of control would move east to the offices of the former Bell Atlantic.

This case is about coaching a leader, Ezra Singer, toward success in a new position as Verizon's highest-ranking HR executive, a position of pivotal importance to the effectiveness of the merger. The fact that he was from GTE, which lost most of its executives in the merger process, caused some speculation about the nature of decisions to come. Would the newly merged entity utilize GTE practices and policies? Many questions like this went through the minds of the employees and the executives. To add to the turmoil, the executives were also operating in a new and unpredictable arena and without many of the networking relationships they had developed over the years.

Many of the exiting executives were coached, and some of those who remained were coached. In the majority of cases, the decision to leave was based on geographic preferences because, for many, moving from the South to the Northeast was not an option. Some took early retirement, which is normal in a merger of this size. For many others, the culture of the new organization did not seem to fit with either their personal or professional goals.

Defining Coaching at Verizon

After exploring the many coaching definitions in programs that were considered best practices in both companies, the coaches sought a common definition. This was the result: "Coaching is about bringing out the best in people, having others be successful, or conveying valued people from where they are now to where they want to go."

Coaching for Ezra Singer was based on a coaching partnership that fostered a determination and clarified a decision for him to take on a key leadership position in this newly forming mega-company. It was about "conveying" him to own the role of executive vice president of HR when his background might have prompted other views.

The Strategy for Coaching

There were several challenges facing Ezra Singer. First, he had moved from managing a group of 15 lawyers to leading a function of approximately 2,000 HR employees. Second, his new leadership team was from both companies, so some divergent views could be expected. Third, as in any merger, there was a period during which people were cautious with decisions and needed to build trust.

The coach focused primarily on Ezra taking on this new role, but also employed a team coaching approach with the HR Leadership Team (HRLT), as a result of the priorities and initiatives Ezra launched within the department in order to support the lines of business.

Ezra had assumed the role of executive vice president of HR less than six months after his appointment to an executive compensation and benefits position within HR. Because his background was in the legal department, Ezra wanted coaching on HR and the associated expectations and culture. The dialogue with Ezra resulted in many coaching opportunities with his entire HR leadership team, as governance processes and collaboration methodologies were defined and enhanced. Ezra met the internal executive coach through the process of planning a surprise birthday party for a coworker, who happened to be the coach's immediate supervisor. Ezra inquired what the coach did with GTE and said he might need some coaching services.

The first coaching opportunity was to conduct one-on-one interviews with the HRLT to ask for suggestions for enhancing the teamwork within the function. The team expressed concerns about the structure of HR, the need to articulate a strategy, and the essential task of establishing the value added by the HR function with its key stakeholders.

The Strategy

The coaching conversations were conducted either in person or over the phone. Initially, the meetings were face-to-face to help develop rapport, evolving into predominantly phone conversations. These coaching relationships were relatively long, two to three years, as the challenges of integrating the former GTE and Bell Atlantic were addressed.

Because the relationship was an internal coaching arrangement, there were no fees or contracts. The agreement was that the coaching relationship would continue through a series of projects and challenges, as long as it was satisfying to the client and measurable results were produced. Key strategic initiatives were identified and tracked, with measurable outcomes.

The Coaching Conversation

The starting point for the coaching relationship was typical for an executive assuming a new role in this type of merger: Ezra's major challenges included managing his time and balancing his work and personal life. Because he had been appointed on an interim basis, Ezra also needed to make a decision about whether or not he wanted the position on a permanent basis.

Access Point

A significant shift in Ezra's thinking came with the realization that failure in the HR role was not an option. He had achieved much success and many financial rewards in his career—so he chose to see this new opportunity as an adventure, rather than a test. He began to enjoy the challenges and to become self-regulating in his own development. He acknowledged incremental changes over time and actively sought feedback from constituents. He reacted to unexpected obstacles with confidence that the combination of his natural intellectual abilities and integrity would guide him in the right direction.

The biggest challenge for some high-ranking executives is the insular nature of their positions: People tend to tell them only good news and what they think the executives want to hear. Ezra was zealous in his quest for open and honest feedback and indeed many times sought out negative or constructive feedback, viewing it as a gift. He specifically asked for feedback in conversations following Business Television broadcasts to HR employees and through electronic surveys. Because he was still developing his image as an HR executive, he did not take the feedback personally, but viewed it as an opportunity for definition and improvement.

Point of Celebration

Ezra became comfortable with the executive vice president role and used his natural wit and humor to set the pace for his interactions. He forged new working relationships with key executives and was successful in standardizing and integrating the policies and processes of the two former companies. He emphasized a total rewards approach to benefits, pension, compensation, and savings. In addition, he utilized a formula of operational excellence, integration, and key strategic initiatives to help accelerate the merger considerations. Throughout this process, he became a trusted and strategic leader.

As an adjunct to the executive coaching, there was an opportunity to coach the leadership team for HR. In addition to preliminary interviews and the benefit of facilitating several strategy sessions with the team, the group set out to achieve more camaraderie among its members by clarifying roles and building goodwill. A governance process was defined and implemented, and communication and coordination between the centers of excellence and the lines of business was enhanced. The increased teamwork improved the HR staff's ability to focus on four strategic initiatives, which are currently being implemented. The four strategic HR initiatives for 2002-2003 include

- enhancing a labor-relations strategy focused on developing the skills of the first-level supervisors when dealing with unionized employees
- creating an e-HR strategy to determine how to utilize the intranet and Internet to facilitate e-learning and e-communication at Verizon
- identifying or branding the employee experience to answer the question of what it is like to work at Verizon, addressing work environment issues, productivity and attendance, culture, coaching, retention, and business direction
- developing key workforce and leadership capabilities in an effort to identify future skill requirements, assess the gaps between current and future skills, and prescribe potential remedies to close the gaps.

The strategic initiative teams have co-leadership roles and represent the lines of business and the centers of excellence to help ensure the practicality and "fit" of the concepts and implementation plans. One way to measure the effectiveness of these strategic initiatives is VZ Viewpoints, the company's employee opinion survey, which is administered twice each year.

Measuring Success

The HR function achieved exemplary results on the employee opinion survey during Ezra's first year as executive vice president. In fact, although the corporation overall experienced a plateau effect in employee perceptions, largely related to downsizing efforts, the HR function experienced significantly increased favorable ratings. Of the 58 items on the survey, 33 showed statistically significant improvement over results for the first quarter of 2001, and 15 of the 33 items improved by 10 or more percentage points.

For instance, one of the most highly scored items (93 percent) was a measure of cooperation to get the job done, indicating teamwork within the function and with stakeholders. The most improved item (17 points), although it remained a challenge, was a measure of the positive dialogue within the organization, with employees making more positive comments about Verizon than six months ago. Another positive and significant change (16-point improvement) was in the service mindset when interacting with "our customers, our communities, and each other."

The fact that the HR function experienced significant positive improvement while the corporation as a whole experienced a plateau effect further distinguished the efforts within the HR function. Table 1 gives more details of specific survey items, which reflect the results from fourth quarter of 2001 for HR.

Several measures of success were used in the coaching evaluation. For HR, stakeholder feedback and employee survey results were used to assess the internal reaction to leadership. For the line of business clients, productivity measures and employee survey results were used as indicators. The HR function also began to link productivity

Table 1. VZ Viewpoints human resources survey results for fourth quarter 2001.

Survey Item	Results
Verizon respects diversity of employees.	94% favorable (+ 10)*
People I work with cooperate to get the job done.	93% favorable (+ 3)
Respond to customers with a sense of urgency.	89% favorable (+ 2)
Committed to Verizon.	88% favorable (+ 5)
Proud to be part of Verizon.	88% favorable (+ 10)
Verizon stock is a good investment.	77% favorable (+ 15)
Deliver on goal to create the most respected brand in communications.	77% favorable (+ 16)
People always willing to give best effort to help company succeed.	77% favorable (+ 12)
We have a service mindset when interacting with customers, our communities, and each other.	77% favorable (+ 16)
Overall satisfaction with Verizon.	74% favorable (+ 11)
Challenges:	
More positive comments about Verizon than six months ago.	35% favorable (+ 17)

*Number in parentheses indicates improvement over first quarter 2001 survey results.

results, for instance, to the quality of the labor relations environment and formed an Employee Engagement Index to identify the key causes or drivers of the survey results. In this way, we established a quantitative link between the line of business goals and the HR strategic initiatives.

Continuous feedback about the perceived value of the coaching relationship was solicited, and adjustments were made over time to accommodate new situations and opportunities. These included after-action reviews, in order to learn from accomplishments and challenges, and facilitating cross-departmental teamwork within HR.

Lessons Learned

From a client perspective, lessons included greater insight and confidence, in addition to measurable and tangible results. Stakeholder feedback is always helpful, and employee survey results measure improvements and variations over time.

From a coaching perspective, lessons included maintaining flexibility around the executive's schedule. Some weeks included three or four conversations, while others involved only one or none. The response time in executive coaching is critical: When the executive needs to discuss a situation, the timeframe is usually short. When situations or priorities occur, the need for just-in-time coaching is apparent. Therefore, having organizational and cultural support for the intensity of coaching was reassuring.

Coaching is an inter-developmental relationship. In providing coaching to highly successful individuals, emphasis on "raising the bar" stimulated the need for continuous improvement in coaching skills, too. Monitoring personal or leadership progress is a constant challenge. For example, the intensity of the questions increased as the coaching relationship evolved. In other words, techniques such as lasering rather than straightforward, direct questions propelled the conversation and action forward most effectively as the coaching relationship progressed. In the beginning, these techniques caused a pause and potentially slowed the action, but as the coaching rhythm developed, the openness to these more assertive techniques increased. Ezra's self-knowledge increased over time, and his openness to challenge himself and identify stretch goals and targets expanded.

The coach must also be on a path of continuous improvement if he or she is to experience a significant shift in the coaching relationship. Abiding concern and respect for the executive is critical to the executive's development of trust and faith that the coach has the executive's best interests at heart at all times, during the coaching experience and beyond. Utilizing the common tools of coaching—including listening, feedback, observations, and questions—is a starting point, but the coach also needs an awareness of current events, technological and political considerations, and cultural challenges or differences.

The case for just-in-time coaching is best made at the executive level. Seizing the opportunities for "coachable moments"—even as planned discussions are scheduled and executed—is exciting and interesting.

Moving from an individual to a team coaching arrangement involves gaining the trust of the team members, even as the coach continues to work with the executive. Confidentiality and intense focus are required.

Knowing the business model and the culture of the organization is a distinct advantage for the internal coach. This knowledge also challenges the coach to constantly question the assumptions and paradigms of the culture, so the envelope is continually pushed and rearranged. Benchmarking with other companies and networking with other coaches also helps provide perspective, as does employing an external mentor coach to help improve focus and determine priorities.

Questions for Discussion
1. What is the definition or context for "just-in-time" coaching?
2. What techniques can or should be used in the beginning of the coaching relationship as opposed to after the relationship has matured?
3. How can an internal executive coach ensure that he or she is sufficiently challenging executive clients?
4. How can the coach help ensure that the executive is not being insulated in his or her communication and feedback?
5. How might internal executive coaching differ from external coaching?
6. Are there specific behaviors and decision points characteristic of mergers that may not occur at other times in the careers of executives?

The Author
Nancy K. Philabaum is the director—workforce and leadership initiatives for Verizon Communications, a merged entity of Bell Atlantic and GTE, with approximately 250,000 employees. In her role, Philabaum provides executive coaching to the managers and executives and is responsible for helping to shape a culture of coaching

within Verizon. In addition, she works with the labor relations and business leaders to help improve the relationship between Verizon management and its two major unions, CWA and IBEW. She is also involved in the four key strategic initiatives for HR for 2002-2003, which include leadership and workforce capability, employee experience, labor relations, and e-HR.

She has worked with GTE and Verizon for 17 years and has a master's degree in speech communication from Southwest Texas State University. Philabaum can be reached at Verizon, 545 E. John Carpenter Freeway, Mailcode HQB09B62, Irving, TX 75062; phone: 972.718.4221; email: nancy.philabaum@verizon.com.

The Power of Conversation: Changing a Company Culture One Executive at a Time

A National Nonprofit Organization

Terrie Lupberger

Experience has taught us that the foundation for change in an organization is the personal transformation of the individuals that constitute it. The confidence, genuineness, respect for others, creativity, spirit, commitment, and faultless performance required by successful organizations is achieved only with the establishment of a learning environment that leads to the development of the individuals whose cooperation and synergy can sustain it and innovate within it.

In this case study a vice president in a national member-driven nonprofit organization was facing significant changes that required him and his senior team to shift not only the roles they played in the organization but also the way they related to each other and the rest of the organization's employees. Through powerful conversations, this vice president was able not only to produce new and more effective actions, but also a greater sense of relatedness with his team and a deeper sense of personal well-being that spilled over into his family life. The conversational space offered by coaching had a profound and transforming impact on his ability to have the needed conversations with those in his organization, conversations that were previously unavailable to him.

Organization Profile

A health-care-related nonprofit organization, headquartered in Washington, D.C., served more than 250,000 members nationwide. For the first time in a decade, the organization was restructuring the

This case was prepared to serve as a basis for discussion rather than to illustrate either effective or ineffective administrative and management practices. Names of places, organizations, or people have been disguised at the request of the author or organization.

relationships of the managers in the field and the managers at headquarters, all to better serve the members. The organization was also laying off some employees and asking others to relocate. Senior management was being asked to take on a new management "style," moving to more of a "consultant" role from that of a "director" role and to change toward a more collaborative and co-creative style of managing and leading.

Background

In addition to offering executive coaching and leadership programs within organizations, the Newfield Network offers public coach training programs in which individuals from any organization can be trained as an internal coach. It was in one of its public coach training programs that a senior HR representative of the nonprofit organization experienced the transforming power of coaching. The HR representative asked the Newfield Network to interview with the organization with the goal of assisting it with some of the changes it was facing.

Coaching is the most potent means presently available for producing lasting organizational change and personal transformation. It is within this framework that the Newfield Network presented a program for supporting the nonprofit organization's change initiative. During the interviewing process, the senior HR official, and Steve, the vice president of operations, spoke about needing to make shifts that required quantum leaps in the traditional ways they had managed and related to each other. Even though Steve did not initially articulate his concern in this way, he felt strongly that their ways of communicating with each other and the membership were insufficient to carry them into this new organizational model while simultaneously meeting their aggressive organizational goals.

In the initial coaching conversations, Steve and the HR director indicated that they would like to address two primary concerns: 1) improve the effectiveness of the team's communication with each other and their subordinates; and 2) model coaching and bring to their work awareness of the distinctions and skills of coaching.

Throughout the extensive interviewing process, it became obvious that the members of this senior-level team were 1) very receptive to new thinking (and quite tired of traditional interventions that had failed to produce lasting change in the past); 2) supported by the top management of the organization; and 3) willing to invest time and energy in this initiative. These three criteria are essential ingredients for successful organizational work or executive coaching initiatives.

With this as background, the coaching team began interviewing the senior managers who made up the company's leadership team. The coaches elicited, through many conversations, what the team members thought were the critical issues to address. The answers fell into three broad categories:

- We recognize that our current ways of working together aren't producing the results we want.
- There is too much work, and our well-being is at stake.
- We aren't honest with each other. When we meet, we posture and politic and roadblock each other, but it's all veiled with great politeness. (Newfield coaches call this "cordial hypocrisy.")

These were the general themes around which the team of coaches began working with the senior leadership team.

Strategy

The profession and field of coaching has yet to powerfully define itself or distinguish itself from other related professions, such as training and consulting. Coaching, as Newfield Network defines it, can be an effective catalyst for change. Coaches, internal and external, need to become powerful observers—of themselves, of others, and of the various systems in which they live and work. The more they can see or observe, the more opportunities they have to intervene or take different actions.

Good coaching increases clients' awareness of how their habitual ways of speaking and moving and their habitual moods and emotions affect their ability to lead, to change, and to learn. In fact, Newfield's teaching methods say that coaching equals learning. Few things in life are more important than learning: It has the power to shape everything we say and do and deeply affects the quality of our lives. Time spent learning is probably the most valuable investment we ever make. We rightly pay great attention to education, especially in youth. Yet we rarely look very deeply into learning itself or ask ourselves what it is, what its goals are, and how it might be changed.

The great challenge and opportunity facing us is to become truly serious about elaborating a new well-grounded, multidimensional discourse on learning, one that can address the fundamentally important questions of what it means to be a human being, how we can live together in harmony with each other and the planet, and how we can coordinate more effective action with each other. Newfield believes these challenges and opportunities called coaching into existence.

Coaching legitimizes and produces conversations in which the accumulation of knowledge for the sake of producing effective action is supported by, and held within, a higher goal of producing wisdom for the sake of effective living. It is within this frame of reference that Steve entered into a coaching relationship.

In the first two meetings with Steve, the coach presented theories and models and discussed with Steve his own goals for the coaching relationship. After these first sessions with his coach, Steve declared that his goal was to increase his capacity and competency to have powerful conversations—conversations that could produce his desired outcomes but which he either didn't know were needed or felt unable to have. In the process, he admitted that he had to learn many things. He had to learn what conversations were missing with his team and the individual members that composed it. He had to learn what those missing conversations were costing him and his team, not only in terms of productivity but also in well-being and satisfaction. Steve had to learn what emotions were needed to support him in having new conversations and he had to build his emotional capacity to have them. Steve, as the leader, also needed to learn how to create powerful contexts for learning and action within his organization. So, the process of coaching focused on Steve becoming a better observer of how his language, emotions, and physical movements (posture, tone, gestures) supported his actions and also limited them.

The coaching, although it directly affected his ability to take action, did not focus on or start with Steve and his coach deciding what "actions" he needed to take. First, he needed to understand his predispositions or habits related to taking action; otherwise, as soon as the coach left he would go back to more of the same behaviors.

The Coaching Conversation

The coach agreed to work with Steve (and the senior leadership team) for a period of four months. The design entailed two off-site retreats with the entire group and face-to-face or phone coaching sessions with the individual team members on a weekly basis, in between the conferences. Experience has proven that bringing all the "coaching clients" together to talk about organizational and individual concerns and to introduce them to the key coaching concepts of leadership is a powerful way to produce results for them individually and as a team.

Steve and his team had the following realizations from their conversations together in those two retreats:

- They began to distinguish their opinions and judgments from the facts of their current situation and saw how their policy-making process was largely based on opinion rather than fact. They discussed the many negative implications this had on productivity, sales (membership), and their identity with their customers.

- They began to see the power of emotions and the need for more emotional intelligence in their leadership of the organization. They got to experience and practice which emotions were conducive to achieving different goals. For example, they saw that to innovate required a mood of speculation and wonder and openness—a mood very different from the one needed to conduct a project status meeting. They also realized that they, as a group, tended to fall into one or two particular moods when they came together: quiet resignation—which for them meant that in the end nothing was really going to be different—and masked resentment that there was more work to be done than any human could possibly do. They saw how the emotional space of the team did not allow the needed conversations to happen.

- They realized as a group how bad they were at making requests of each other. They gave no "conditions" for being satisfied (like timeframes) and they gave each other absolutely no room to say no to any request. (This, by the way, is the classic recipe for an overwhelming environment, which was the biggest complaint this team had.)

Through the coaching process at the two retreats, the team was introduced to a new interpretation of communication—the role of the body and emotions in the learning process—for the purpose of improving their ability to coordinate effective action and to better listen to the opportunities that were offered to the organization by its members.

Coaching Steve

Steve was the vice president and the number three person in the organization. When the project began, Steve believed that he was too authoritarian in his leadership style, that he didn't seek enough input or collaboration from his team. During the coaching relationship, Steve eventually revealed that he had always been, in his opinion, a "mediocre" student. He hadn't gone to the best schools or colleges, and his grades had been average (mostly Bs and Cs). In fact, he was surprised by the success he had had in his business life, but was ultimately afraid that if he didn't work hard enough, someone would "find out" how average he was.

Access Point

The coach offered Steve a conversational space in which he could see that his desire to "not be found out" drove him to work hard, to work his team hard, and to be unavailable to listen to his team when they had alternate solutions, feedback, or criticism. Steve's declaration in the coaching relationship was to begin having the important conversations with his team members that he knew were sorely missing. But it wasn't just a matter of having this intellectual realization and then being able to move to the new action—it never is. In working with his coach, Steve had to develop the emotional and physical capacity to have these conversations. He had to build his emotional muscles to withstand constructive criticism and to have a difficult conversation without immediately reacting in anger.

Interestingly, Steve's team did not share his assessment that he was too "authoritarian." They believed that Steve was a very likeable guy. In large part, the team regarded him as a kind father figure. They understood that he was under a great deal of pressure, given the rapid changes the organization was going through. He didn't talk about his stress or concerns with the team, but both were obvious.

In the group coaching conversations, the team admitted that they felt they couldn't say no to him, that they wanted to support him and the organization, very often at the cost of their own well-being. This leadership group cared deeply about their work and the mission of the organization. They cared so much, in fact, that they did not decline any requests from Steve. They were absolutely overwhelmed with work, and costly mistakes were being made—not only in financial terms, but also in the health of the working relationships.

Through the coaching process, Steve came to realize that his stoicism and inability to reveal his own emotions (such as feeling overwhelmed, frustrated, or doubtful) and his incompetence or lack of confidence in his ability to have thoughtful and exploratory conversations with his team were costing him and the team well-being, productivity, and effectiveness.

Point of Action

Through the coaching he received in the group and individually, Steve was able not only to see the habitual patterns of the way he related to his team but also to design new practices with his coach to increase his conversational competency (which required a shift in his emotions and in his body).

Steve's coach kept encouraging him to reflect on several key questions during the relationship:

- What conversations are missing with (team member)?
- What emotions would be needed to have and hold those conversations?
- What practices can we design together to build that emotional competency?
- What haven't you acknowledged or praised about (team member)?
- How do you think this missing conversation is affecting your relationship with him or her?

Point of Celebration

By the end of the final retreat, Steve was a different leader—he was frank, thoughtful, and more able to express his gratitude, as well as his mandates, to his team. There was another wonderful by-product of his ability to express himself—the coaching team called it "lightness." Steve's ability to laugh at himself and with his team was noticeably improved. Steve even led the new tradition of dancing at the end of the program.

Measuring Success

At the beginning of the program, the coach had asked Steve and each team member what they wanted to learn in this program and through the coaching. Although that changed over time for all of them, as it typically does, the coaches checked in with Steve and each of his senior team members at the end of the four months and asked if they were satisfied with the learning that they had produced for themselves in this program.

Although the specific lessons were different for each of them, the results of the conversations were similar: Steve and the team were surprised that in such a short time they could learn so much that had such significant impact in their day-to-day activities. Far more than learning a technique for "better management," they had learned the art of having powerful conversations.

The coach also interviewed the HR director at the end of the project and asked these questions:

- What results do you see or expect to see in your organization from this work?
- What ways of working together do you see as different in this organization now?
- What do you speculate those changes will lead to in terms of productivity, satisfaction, and well-being?

Newfield also followed up with Steve three months later. The coaches were curious about the challenges the team faced when they went back into the system without having the support of coaching on a frequent basis. The coaches were also curious about what practices they could help the team build into their routines and processes.

Unfortunately, many organizations ascribe solely to a scientific world view that in essence says that "if you can't measure it objectively, it doesn't exist." Operating from this view, they won't consider goals that can't be measured scientifically and objectively. This way of seeing the world is slowly changing, but we need new methods for "observing and measuring" and also a respect for such goals as increased meaning, well-being, dignity, love, respect, and commitment.

The coaches could (and did) ask the clients if their sense of well-being had increased; for example, if they were able to have more powerful conversations within the organization (and how that affected their results) and if the way they engaged with their colleagues had improved the organizational mood. In the end, both the coaches and Steve and his team would declare satisfaction with the program and its outcomes. The coaching process had provided the team with, above all else, a very safe learning space and a powerful context in which they could have meaningful conversations.

Lessons Learned
Addressing the "I'm too Busy" Roadblocks

The coaches have found over time that if there is going to be a shift in an organization toward developing authentic practices, it must begin with management—those who direct the employees of the organization toward the common goals. Managers are usually "too busy" to put their attention to serious learning that is not content-focused.

In today's management culture, time is measured in calendar quarters, and for most managers, who have an operational focus, even this increment can seem too long. Quarterly measures may be legitimate for examining financial and production results, but they are useless in charting career and competency development. If a manager charts out a career plan and sees that his or her working life is likely to go on for another 10 or 20 years, the idea of spending a year or more learning new competencies doesn't appear to be unreasonable. This is particularly true when it's overlaid with the increasing pace of change and the pressing obsolescence of existing skills. If a manager is stuck in an operational mindset and is only willing to focus on the next two or three months, the idea of engaging a coach to help produce some substantial changes and develop new competencies will most likely seem an unnecessary and unacceptable addition to an already impossible schedule.

It was difficult to break the belief that "I don't have enough time." Initially the clients frequently broke their coaching appointments, and the coaches found themselves having to track down clients to coach them. When the coaching conversations happened, the leaders reported positive results, but breaking the cultural and organizational conversation called "I'm too busy" required the coaches to be extremely proactive and dogged. The coaches brought this to the team's attention as an organizational "enemy of learning" and gave them the chance to discuss what this was costing in other areas of the organization.

The coaches also reduced the amount of reading and "homework" they gave within the program. In retrospect, they had been too optimistic that the senior leadership team would devote a great deal of energy and time to making the changes that they had called on the coaches to help them make. The coaches consistently find this in most of their work. Our culture wants answers, how-tos, learning sound bites, and quick solutions. The paradox, as mentioned earlier, is that it is only through a different approach to and context for learning that we will come up with the solutions we so desperately want. Otherwise, we will just keep producing more of the same.

Getting an Admission that "I Need Help"

One hurdle on this project was getting Steve and the team of senior leaders to admit they needed help. Newfield calls this "declaring the breakdown." Operating in a mode of "cordial hypocrisy," the team felt that to acknowledge their problems or concerns was to somehow betray or invalidate all the work they had done as an organization to that point. They also genuinely liked each other and felt that any criticism was a personal attack on someone or someone's idea.

The leadership team and coaches had many conversations as a group and individually to convince the group that a declaration of breakdown actually opens new possibilities. It is not until a leader declares that something isn't working that the organization or team can begin looking for solutions or innovations. The coaches insisted that it is a responsibility of a good leader to declare when something isn't working, even when he or she has no idea what the solution may be.

Using Assessment Tools

The Newfield Network is very mindful in their use of assessment tools. Newfield coaches have found that great questioning can reveal more than an assessment tool; that individuals tend to receive the "results" of an assessment tool as if it were "truth" and not just an opinion (which can have very limiting consequences); and that the administrator of the assessment tool can be lulled into a false sense of thinking that he or she "knows" the client. Assessment tools can categorize and generalize, which is in opposition to what great coaches do. On the other hand, in some instances and work cultures, the use of an assessment tool can bring credibility to the initiative, provide a context for the coaching, and offer the coaching client additional insights into how they "show up" for others around them.

In this case, it was agreed that we would not use a particular assessment tool. It was difficult at first to get the client to buy in to this. In the past four years the organization had spent an enormous amount of money on three different tools to assess their communication and leadership strengths and weaknesses. However, about three weeks into the contract negotiations, Steve finally admitted that although the assessment results had been "interesting," they had not produced any real shifts in the way people communicated and related to each other. It was then decided that doing another assessment might actually send the wrong message, one of "we're doing more of the same," and not set the appropriate context for this new initiative.

Coaching Works

Through the outstanding work Steve and his team did in this coaching program, it became apparent once again that the power of coaching lies in creating a learning context in which people can uncover the assumptions that are preventing them from achieving their desired outcomes. A common enemy of coaching is that coaches feel they need to "produce results" for the client in order to be assessed positively. Quite the opposite is true with great coaching: The simple yet profound job of the coach is to create a space or context in which clients themselves can produce results.

Questions for Discussion

1. As a coach, are there situations in which you see yourself rushing to get the client into new action?

2. What do you need to learn to be able to work in a coaching relationship without having to rush to action or provide results for your client?

3. How do you bring the subject of emotional intelligence to your clients?

4. What practices do you design with your clients to build their emotional competency?

5. What resistance do you typically meet in your own corporate clients and what do you need to learn to be able to turn that resistance into even more powerful coaching conversations?

The Author

Terrie Lupberger is the CEO of the Newfield Network. She is a master certified coach through the International Coach Federation and has been coaching executives and other individuals since 1994. She also is presently serving a three-year term as a board member of the International Coach Federation.

Prior to her career at Newfield, Lupberger was a senior partner at a consulting firm that specialized in teaching consulting skills to internal consultants. Their programs taught professionals how to be more influential in partnership with their internal and external clients.

Lupberger's earlier career was spent at the Department of the Treasury where she was a senior financial systems analyst working with the Federal Reserve Banks across the country. She was also a senior manager with the U.S. courts, helping to improve the operations of the district and circuit court system.

Lupberger now leads Newfield's executive coaching team, which has worked directly with thousands of people in nine different countries for the past 18 years. The Newfield team has delivered public and private programs for corporations and organizations throughout the world in the areas of leadership, coaching, and culture change. She can be reached at the Newfield Network, 2804 Fountain Grove, Olney, MD 20832; phone: 301.570.6680; email: terrie@newfieldnetwork.com.

The Extraordinary Game:
The Case for Extreme Team Coaching

Grand Pharmaceuticals

Darelyn "DJ" Mitsch

This case study showcases the dramatic impact of a team-coaching program implemented by a regional sales team in a large international pharmaceutical company. The team moved from fifth rank in its division to second rank within just 16 weeks—one reporting period—through a trademarked coaching program called The Extraordinary Game. The unique elements of this coaching process helped the team focus on a business goal while the coaching duo worked on the team's interpersonal dynamics. The coaching program was highly successful: The team became number one in the United States within eight months—less than two reporting periods—and its members developed new collegial relationships still present today. The return-on-investment (ROI) went beyond the $12 million in new revenues over plan: The team members became aligned as a group of people who could speak their minds and sustain a high level of performance that would create personal legacies.

Organizational Profile

Grand Pharmaceuticals is an international drug company focused on the research and development of respiratory and other prescription drugs. Grand operates in more than 70 countries, but is based primarily in Europe and North and South America. The company has grown to a dominant global position over the past 20 years through launching and patenting innovative medicines and investing in the discovery of new therapies.

This case was prepared to serve as a basis for discussion rather than to illustrate either effective or ineffective administrative and management practices. Names of places, organizations, or people have been disguised at the request of the author or organization.

The 100-year-old company's growth spurt occurred during the early 1980s when it changed its focus from over-the-counter treatments to innovative pharmacology. In a field of thousands of internationally recognized pharmaceutical companies, growing significant shares of revenue and increasing brand recognition depends on more than brilliant business strategies. Growing into a global leader requires a focused attention to hiring, developing, and retaining key leadership and talent. This has been the focus of the company's leadership development programs during recent years.

Background

William, a newly assigned regional manager, had inherited a team of 12 district managers with mixed loyalties and commitments. There were huge communications problems within the team; for example, two of the managers had not spoken to each other for almost two years, and others were hostile toward the marketing manager, who constantly was forced to defend his actions. There were also two camps of district managers, one that welcomed William as the new regional manager and one that aligned with the former manager, who had recently taken a new job within the company. William's primary goals were to get the district managers to talk candidly in order to resolve their differences and to achieve a leading sales rank in the company. His personal business goal was to move up one rank and share within one year, from fifth to fourth.

By the time William had been on the job two weeks he saw why his sales team had such a negative reputation within the company and that the challenges he had thought were blown out of proportion during the interviewing process were very real. As a result, he sought help through the company's HR representative for his area. She recommended that he interview coaches to help him deal with the challenges, naming the Pyramid Resource Group as one possibility. William met with Pyramid for less than an hour and determined that coaching could be a great application, both for him personally and for the group.

The scope of work with William's team included several components, which were laid out in a pre-game blueprint:

- pre-game assessment
- game creation
- coaching
- celebration.

Pre-game Assessment

Over about two weeks, a 20-question assessment was conducted with each of the 12 managers to develop working themes for a game. The resulting report was sanitized to eliminate a trail of identification for any individual. The themes were then shared with William as a part of his personal coaching plan and as the foundation for the team's game creation.

Game Creation

An off-site workshop was designed to allow the team to create a game around the goal of moving up a rank and share within the coming year. This gave the team ownership of the goal in a new way, as the members stretched the company's annual plan for the region by setting "extreme" goals and began playing for higher stakes. Once the rank and share goal—"to move up one rank and share within the next 12 months as a result of the actions taken in the next four"—was set, the team divided the management responsibilities into four product sales increases related to their business plan for the coming year. Each manager teamed with those who shared similar responsibilities or overlapping geographies to create a strategic plan for their sales teams. The two managers who had not spoken in a while ended up on the same team and had to collaborate on assigning points to be scored by their sales teams for one of the product categories

During the two days, the team worked with the coaches to create a strategic game plan. Points were assigned to each of the goals, with a total of 100 points to be scored over the next 16 weeks during the coaching phase of the game. A team charter was created, with agreements for team conduct. The team agreed

- to stop withholding communication and start being straight with each other
- to represent other teammates well within the company outside the peer group
- to stop gossiping
- to stay in the game even when other demands were made on their time
- to remain coachable
- to allow each other some room to make mistakes.

Participants also signed a contract with the two Pyramid coaches that set the stage for their coaching work. During their facilitation of the two-day kickoff workshop, the coaches also witnessed a turning point, a moment of truth from two simple questions they posed on the first day: "What do others say about you as a group? What legacy have you established for yourselves and your sales people?" The team members knew what people thought and were aware of how their behaviors were interpreted and the impact these perceptions had on their sales performers. After a period of reflection, they claimed responsibility for the negative perceptions of the group and declared that it was time to change them. From that candid conversation they vowed to come together as a team and change the way they behaved, communicated, and performed. This declaration shifted the entire context of the work. It was easy later to go back to those same questions in the team coaching and ask them, "What is the legacy you are creating now?" to keep them on track when they lapsed into old patterns of behavior or communication.

The team began an inquiry into how they could become more collaborative. They were thoughtful and deliberate about changing the team's perceptions within the company. The combative energies of the group were transformed into an open contribution and commitment to the mandate to deliver their goals and re-engage as a team. It was holiday time in New York City and there was a hint of magic in the air. Without realizing it, they had committed to winning a much bigger game than what they created on paper.

Coaching

The game worked for two reasons. First, there was a business game created by the team, so they had complete ownership and the focus of the work was on something they needed and wanted to do. Second, the coaching process held the team accountable for keeping their agreements and taking actions necessary to move the team to a new level. The coaching included three components:

- pre-session forms from participants to update the coaches on activities and accomplishments
- participation in the weekly group teleconference coaching sessions to update and score the game and to learn from insights occurring in the team dynamic
- sideline coaching for participants between sessions as needed.

The coaching component of this program is the missing link in having a team-building program hold together beyond the first week after the main event. Many team-building programs stop short of a true partnership, but the coaching sessions in this program became the focus for the team accomplishing weekly actions declared at the end of each teleconference.

Celebration

The last component of the game was celebration. The coaches looked for things to acknowledge during each conference call, but the team had to learn to celebrate their daily wins. This took many forms. They sent each other small gifts. William sent surprises to the sales people as a group for best efforts and to individuals when they did something beyond what was expected. The managers sent gift certificates for dinners to spouses of sales representatives who had worked long hours. There was a lot of hoopla, which in turn created momentum. The new energy was easy to feel and recognize.

At the end of the 16 weeks, the team met for a celebration dinner at a nationally known five-star restaurant. As they acknowledged each other, the feeling of magic from the kickoff in New York was rekindled. The two managers who had taken on more responsibility sat across from each other. They spoke from their hearts as they acknowledged their growing respect and friendship for each other and their appreciation of the representatives' contributions.

William read the rank and share report aloud at dinner. The team had moved from number five in the country to number two. They were poised to take the number one position in the next trimester, and indeed they called Pyramid Resource Group upon receipt of the second trimester report and excitedly explained that they had reached the number one position.

William had been accepted by his new team in a very short period of time. Industry standards indicate it takes about 18 months to two years to fully assimilate a new manager in a sales territory like this one. Because of the results of the Extraordinary Game, and the team's movement from fifth to first rank within five months, William became the company's newest franchise player—a much sought-after thought leader and—to some—a hero. He had taken a tough assignment and achieved the extraordinary in a very short time.

Overcoming Challenges

Two major events created challenges for the team during the coaching period. First, two senior managers on William's team were asked to leave the company because of questionable conduct, and their sales teams had to be moved to interim management. The two managers who volunteered to manage these sales teams were the two who had not been on good terms prior to the game. Although a competition for recognition fueled their actions, there was also a sense of senior leadership present in their behaviors. They understood that they indirectly affected the work of the team through what they said and did.

As their management workload doubled, the two found they needed to rely on each other and share information to bring these orphaned districts into the game. Without the focus of these critical sales teams on the game, the game points could not be scored and the game would be lost. The coaches also had to learn to avoid being drawn into the drama of the larger changes taking place within the company and let the team off the hook. The coaches' focus was on holding the team accountable for winning the game it had created.

The second challenge during this time came when the Federal Drug Administration postponed one of the products scheduled for launch in the United States. This problem was quickly addressed by refocusing attention on the two heritage therapies from which the new drug had been formulated. Having the construct of a game in place helped the team to remain flexible in their planning and execution strategies, as the managers learned that they could adjust to a changing market while retaining their attention on the overall game plan. Because of the construct of a game, and their agreement with teammates to stay focused even when other priorities surfaced, they realized the value of becoming flexible in changing goals and reassigning priorities when old goals or mandates were no longer valuable. Although many of the game goals remained the same throughout the 16 weeks, several had to be adjusted to accommodate the marketplace. Without the construct of the game, some of the original goals could have easily been overlooked as the team rushed to address the new concerns presented by the ruling change of the FDA.

Measuring Success

The total cost of the program, including individual coaching for the two managers, was about $54,000, which included coaching for William through the process. The increases realized in rank and share had a net result of about $12 million in revenue above plan across four months. Because no ROI study was performed, there is no way to determine what other factors affected the success of the program, but the client's opinion was enough for the coaches: "This was phenomenal. These results are unprecedented in our company. Our folks have accomplished what industry experts contend it takes two years to build—a solid team approach."

To a coach, this praise is worth as much as the bottom-line impact is to the company.

The company was engaged in a new mega-merger a year later. Because the Extraordinary Game was given the highest confidence rating as a best practice by the district managers, several other regions engaged the coaches to conduct games during the merger process.

Discoveries

Coaches operate in a mode of inquiry and learning. There were as many lessons for the coaches as there were for the team. Here are the highlights:

- *Coaching a team requires the coach to become a full partner who can speak as more than a group facilitator.* The role of the team's coach during the game is to request reflection, challenge assumptions, and offer perspective. It sometimes is easier for the coach to just facilitate the flow of dialogue without interrupting the action, but the real power lies in the coach becoming a model for a straight-talk approach. This leads to significant change.
- *It is easy to become embroiled in the drama of the company's market conditions or internal politics.* Detachment is the key to staying in the coaching role and offering perspective when someone declares market forces or politics as reasons for not reaching the game's goal.
- *At some point in the game the participants will always find fault with the coaches.* People often resist or disagree when challenged to think in new ways. This happened most often during the game when the coaches asked the team members, who viewed themselves as victims, to take full ownership of the changes they needed to make. During week four, several people asked if the coaches could reduce the number of phone calls. Many wanted to change the game rules, the ones they themselves had made up and agreed to at the outset of the game. Pyramid has found over the course of many games that people habitually look outside themselves to blame someone or something for failures. As a society, we need to revisit the idea of failing as a normal part of the path to success. When this group started to take full responsibility for winning the game, they started functioning as a cohesive team. In the end the coaches were partners and heroes, but the coaches had to trust the rigorous process and the power of coaching to traverse the rough spots during the 16 weeks.
- *The coaches could not know the end result.* Playing the Extraordinary Game is like playing sports: If the focus is on the scoreboard, the team could miss the chance to take the bold actions that actually lead to winning. The coaches wanted to stay focused on accelerating performance;

they trusted that if they continued to coach the plays—the weekly actions the team took—the team would find a way to score the points. The coach cannot play the game or score the points, the team has to do it.

- *In the context of playing the game, people tend to act like they act at work every day.* The power of playing the game lies in allowing people to see interactions and conversations from a new vantage point. They can more easily become observers when it is "just a game" they are playing. From that perspective, they learn to coach themselves.

- *The coaches learned that the team has a unique voice.* Most corporate coaches work one-on-one with executives. The power in this group coaching experience came from hearing these district manager's combined messages as if they spoke with one voice. It allowed the coaches to coach the team as they would have coached an individual and to get at the root cause of the breakdowns in performance they had experienced.

Conclusion

Playing the Extraordinary Game proved to be a provocative way to accelerate growth for this pharmaceutical sales team. There were several success factors for this coaching initiative:

- The coaches were full partners with William. He relied on them to help sift through the tough spots and was personally very open to the coaching.

- William also allowed the coaches to stay in the process of inquiry instead of exerting his control when they asked tough questions.

- The periods of quiet reflection during the kickoff session and the teleconferences were important for the team's growth. This reflective state made participants uncomfortable at first.

- The managers wanted to fill the space with conversation, but learned the value of soul searching and reflection.

- Having a concrete business goal or business rationale was critical in order for this team to gain some traction. The company had a great reputation for professional development, but a link between what they already knew how to do and the coaching was needed. The game gave them the link.

Although the Extraordinary Game was listed by the company as a best practice, it was also a secret weapon. Once the idea spread, William and the others who had done this early in their team development became reluctant to share the idea with others who could use the same process to take back the leadership ranks. One of Pyramid's key lessons was that the firm may only be able to do one of these engagements for a client company in which there is competition among divisions. But imagine what would happen if all regions played a big game: Market dominance might really be possible. Unfortunately, every top performer eventually asks, "Who wants to give up being number one?"

Questions for Discussion

1. How can playing a game address the HR development needs apparent in new team startups or new manager assimilations?
2. Executives are always looking for a bottom-line impact in HR development. Discuss three to five needs that corporate teams could address by using a "game" concept.
3. What is the value of having a coach partner with a new manager to help integrate his or her leadership style when taking over a veteran management team?
4. How can playing a game keep managers focused on the meaningful actions that drive the score instead of focusing only on the scoreboard?
5. What is the importance of celebration throughout the course of a sales team's performance?
6. How is coaching applied for a business team in much the same way as it is for a sports organization?

The Author

Darelyn "DJ" Mitsch is an executive coach and author, and president of the Pyramid Resource Group, The Corporate Coaching Company. A pioneer in coaching and a master certified coach through the International Coach Federation, she served as a board member from 1999 through 2002, and as the professional society's president in 2001, where she expanded the dynamic society to global service. She creates innovative coaching programs and develops strategies for leaders and their companies, those who are up to playing a big game in the world. Mitsch has a 16-year background in broadcast management, where she was a vice president and general manager reporting to a board of directors. Mitsch is currently researching, writing, and speaking for associations and firms on topics of leadership development and supporting leaders to live authentic, balanced, and rewarding lives. She can be reached by phone: 919.677.9300; email: dj@pyramidresource.com. Her Website is at www.pyramidresource.com.

Constructing a Life
While Building a Business

Bob's Construction Company

Douglas A. Leland

In less than three years, the president of a construction company turned a barely surviving business into a thriving company by focusing on his personal life. From long and frustrating days at work to extended vacations and short workweeks, this president's emphasis on balance led to a tripling of revenues and profits, personal prosperity, and a major leap toward financial independence. Through a one-on-one, face-to-face coaching partnership and the balancing of personal needs with professional aspirations, this president grew his company in size, profitability, sophistication, efficiency, and competitiveness by taking better care of himself and spending more time with his family. This story demonstrates the power of coaching and life balance to change lives, companies, and communities.

Background

Bob is president and owner of a construction company with annual revenues exceeding $5 million. He left the corporate world in his mid-twenties to start his own company. Although Bob is not a corporate executive, his coach has learned that objectives and issues vary little from corporate managers and executives to small business owners. In Bob's case, the primary objective was a desire for a more balanced life. During the four years Bob worked with his coach, he achieved his first two objectives—balance and financial prosperity. His current objectives are attaining financial independence and identifying his unique purpose in life.

This case was prepared to serve as a basis for discussion rather than to illustrate either effective or ineffective administrative and management practices. Names of places, organization, or people have been disguised at the request of the author or organization.

In the early 1990s, Bob left a large accounting firm, where he was a CPA, to start his own business in a field in which he had no experience: construction. He was married and about to start a family. His business began as a partnership with a friend, and his first job was to build a fence for $1,000. When Bob's coaching began, his partner had recently and abruptly left the business, which resulted in substantial debt for Bob and a huge void in construction experience and expertise. Business growth was slow, office morale was low, and Bob was spending more and more time at work with decreasing returns. Although no aspect of his personal or professional life was yet in crisis, he could see the direction in which both were heading and decided to make some changes. At the time, Bob's coach was beginning his coaching business and sought a few people with whom he could work for two months on a pro bono basis. Two of the many characteristics that have made Bob so successful are his alertness to opportunity and openness to new possibilities. When he learned of the coach's need for clients, Bob volunteered, and the two have been working together ever since.

Strategy

Coaching is a partnership based on honesty, trust, and mutual respect that is designed to support the attainment of objectives with ease, grace, and effectiveness while maintaining integrity and alignment with core values. Although every coaching partnership is unique, any time a component is missing, the effectiveness of the relationship is diminished. In some cases, this may call into question the advisability of continuing the relationship.

The Coaching Process

Bob's primary objective was "balance." More specifically, he wanted to spend more time with his family. He stated that his business was fine, other than being demanding of his time. Over his objections, his coach began by focusing on Bob's business—after all, that's where he was spending most of his time. The void created by his partner's departure had created stress, especially in regard to finances and a need to fill the operational and construction expertise gaps. Bob had taught himself what he needed to know regarding operations, gained construction expertise, and pushed his business forward with the tenacity of a bulldog. The combination of stress and filling this void caused Bob to focus on details and control all aspects of the business, including his people, and to push the business forward with brute strength. He began doing more and more, and the smothering environment caused his employees to do less and less. More important, Bob was doing more of what he didn't enjoy doing—operations—and less of what he had enjoyed—selling and business development. The initial strategy for achieving balance was to begin restructuring the business so Bob could devote more energy to growing the business and less to operations.

Best Practices

In terms of strategy, several best practices were employed:

- *Assessments.* Two assessment questionnaires were used at the very beginning of the coaching partnership in order to create context for the relationship, establish priorities, set objectives, and initiate discussions. Objectives changed over time, but these tools helped to provide a starting point and to uncover a few obstacles.
- *Field Work.* Bob enjoys structure and tasks. Used appropriately, task assignments allowed Bob to break big issues into smaller ones and then to explore them more deeply. Using the Personal Foundation Program, a Coach U assessment tool, as a backdrop to the coaching partnership, Bob was able to explore such areas as strengths, needs, values, family, and money at the same time that the coaching conversations wove these concepts into his current professional and personal activities.
- *Ideal Client.* Bob's coach asked him to identify the characteristics of his ideal clients and then to begin to do business only with those meeting these criteria. It took a while for Bob to fully understand and integrate this concept into his business, but once he had, operational problems began to decrease (freeing more time for Bob to pursue business development) and customer satisfaction began to increase, along with profitability.
- *Listening.* Bob learns best by talking, which required his coach to be very comfortable with doing a lot of listening. It was not unusual for Bob to talk for most of the coaching session or one hour, with the discussion guided by a few key questions, comments, and requests from the coach.
- *Raise the Bar.* Bob is energetic, confident, competitive, and responsible. Helping him step out of the details in order to see the big picture also allowed him to see where he could raise the bar. Once the bar was reset, Bob would enthusiastically go about the business of reaching his new standards.

Agreements

Before getting started, Bob completed a coaching agreement, which outlined meeting times, frequency, location, and duration. It also addressed fee structure, payment policies, expectations of each other, and confidentiality. It was not a legal contract, and both parties could disengage at any time. One of the cornerstone verbal agreements between Bob and his coach was that both would be absolutely honest and unconditionally constructive with one another. This alone determined to a great extent the success of this coaching partnership.

The Coaching Conversation

Although the coach's typical coaching sessions take place almost exclusively over the telephone, physical proximity allowed his sessions with Bob to take place in person. They arranged to meet three times a month for 45 to 60 minutes.

At this writing, Bob has advanced through two significant stages of development and has just entered a third. The objectives of the first stage were to stabilize his business and achieve personal balance. The second stage focused on building financial reserves and being financially independent by age 45; that is, no need for any additional income after age 45. The third stage is to achieve fulfillment by identifying the unique purpose for which he was brought into the world and to align his talents, skills, values, activities, and energies accordingly.

The first stage, achieving balance, required Bob to step out of his comfort zone, change behaviors, and take actions based on faith rather than logic. In his determination to make his business successful, he was micromanaging his employees, which further removed him from his business objectives and his family. Within the first month of coaching, the coach asked Bob to take a one-week vacation with his family. During this week he was not to access email or have any contact with his office. Very reluctantly, he agreed. The Monday he returned he was asked whether the business had operated adequately in his absence. The answer was "yes." Bob was then asked to take the rest of the week off, during which he was allowed to contact existing clients and prospective clients, but not to go to his office. After the two-week break, Bob realized that others could handle the day-to-day details and that his talents could be better utilized elsewhere.

During the next year, Bob restructured his business and placed others in charge of the activities he least enjoyed. He freed himself for the critical aspects of the business about which he was most passionate:

selling, growing the business, taking care of customers, and mapping out longer-term objectives for the company.

While achieving this balance, Bob demonstrated that making money and growing a profitable business were not difficult for him. Bob is truly talented when it comes to attracting new business: At the end of the first year of coaching, Bob had doubled the company's revenue and nearly doubled profits. Revenue increased another 50 percent the following year. In addition, Bob has reduced his workweek to four days and consistently takes six weeks of scheduled vacation each year. He has eliminated unwanted obligations and replaced them with activities that allow him to spend more time each week with his children and wife.

The second stage of coaching, achieving financial independence, began about six months into the coaching relationship. Through the frustration that was apparent in Bob's words and demeanor, a huge problem surfaced: As fast as he could make money, his wife was spending it. Although he was genuinely confident that he could always increase his income, he could not see getting ahead if at the end of his efforts there was no net gain. Bob and his wife had different relationships with money: Bob could answer the question "how much is enough?" but his wife could not. Bob wanted to be financially independent by 45 and knew that it would never happen if spending continued to keep pace with his income. He was reluctant to force a resolution of this issue—it created too much disharmony, and his marriage was his top priority.

The turning point came when Bob was told that his marriage would fail if he didn't confront and resolve this issue. It took time, constructive conversation, research, guidance from a variety of financial planners, and some give-and-take, but in the end, both partners agreed on "how much was enough." They established a financial plan that maintained their current lifestyle and also satisfied needs for college tuition, retirement planning, and savings. Establishing a spending ceiling put Bob in a position to contribute all "excess" income toward his financial independence objective. Most important, honest communication resolved a deep-seated frustration that was eroding the most important aspects of his life: his marriage and family. During the past three years Bob's spending ceiling has not changed, but his income has increased 200 percent.

Bob is a talented, confident, effective, and engaging leader who contributes significant time and talent in the service of others. He believes he has a calling that transcends the significant level of contribution he is currently making and he intends to more clearly define it and align his life accordingly. A student of many things, Bob is currently enrolled in a one-year program designed to assist him in achieving this objective.

Measuring Success

There are at least two significant and varying perspectives regarding the value of coaching, each relying on a different set of measurements. The first is the perspective of the individual engaged in the coaching relationship; the second is that of the corporation or corporate decision makers who sponsor coaching engagements but are not participants themselves—the experiential perspective versus the conceptual perspective.

Bob represents both perspectives: Once someone has experienced coaching, his or her perspective would primarily be that of the participant and less that of the corporate decision maker. Those who experience coaching understand that there will never be a return-on-investment (ROI) measurement that adequately captures the value they have received. As a result, they are much more comfortable with "softer" measurements and accept the words of the participants and personal observations of change as sufficient endorsement. Those who have not experienced coaching must and do rely on formulas, which are helpful in documenting financial value but fail to capture the entire financial and organizational impact.

In Bob's case, a few of the objective results to date include

- tripling corporate revenue in four years
- tripling corporate profit in four years
- tripling personal income in four years
- reducing personal workweek to four days
- increasing personal scheduled annual vacation to six weeks
- creating three new companies
- significantly increased long-term financial reserves.

As Bob noted in a letter he wrote to his coach, he began to realize that the value of his coaching experience goes beyond objective measures: "I now see that life is not one accomplishment after another, always trying to get things done, but a journey that we are to experience in the moment. I can now take away the excuses of not having enough time or money to achieve my goals and get rid of the incompletions in my life to free up energy and time to do what fulfills me."

None of Bob's plans for the future state in specific terms the objective ROI-type of improvements that resulted during the period he has been engaged in his coaching partnership. Once coaching is experienced, the criteria for measurement shift more to those of internal rather than external value. In terms of individual coaching relationships, another key measurement of value is the client's decision to continue the coaching partnership. In most cases these relationships run from month to month, with no contractual requirement or incentive to continue beyond the current month. In other words, individuals engaged in coaching partnerships conduct their own internal ROI analysis every month. In many cases, long-term relationships not only suggest that the client's criteria for value have been satisfied, but also that the initial objectives were achieved and new objectives have taken their place.

Corporate executives who make decisions regarding the implementation of coaching programs in the absence of personal experience with coaching will understandably seek objective "proof" of the value of coaching in order to support their decision to expend corporate resources. One of the most definitive ROI studies conducted to date regarding the value of coaching programs within a corporate environment was the Leadership Edge Coaching Study completed by MetrixGlobal in 2001 on behalf of the Pyramid Resource Group and Nortel Networks. The results confirm the substantial financial benefits of coaching interventions and establish a methodology that can be replicated to further evaluate coaching programs going forward. The second chapter of this book covers the coaching program at Nortel Networks and the results of this study.

Lessons Learned

Coaching is truly a partnership, and Bob was not the only one to benefit from the partnership: His coach made numerous discoveries and learned many lessons during his work with Bob. The lessons learned or reinforced through partnering with Bob are ones that surface in most coaching relationships and further demonstrate the important distinction between "simple" and "easy": Much of life is simple, just not easy.

A few of the lessons learned or reinforced were the following:
- *Hold clients accountable.* Until they take responsibility for every aspect and situation in their lives, progress will be limited.
- *Listen rather than advise.* Clients learn by discovering their own wisdom, not by hearing that of the coach. Bob's coach had to overcome

a belief that he needed to talk in order to justify his invoice; the opposite is actually true. With Bob, who learns best by talking himself through issues, the coach had to learn to patiently listen in order to see the big picture and identify opportunities to "raise the bar."

- *Raise the bar.* Living a life in which you consistently raise your standards is not easy, but this is a requirement in long-term coaching relationships. Partnering with Bob taught the coach to see stages in development, valleys and plateaus, and opportunities to tackle new peaks. He learned to identify the incremental nature of coaching and to be comfortable with patience. Increasing goals can be exhilarating, but isn't always easy. It's OK to rest between reaching the peaks.

- *Only work with ideal clients.* As the coach worked with Bob to define his ideal client and supported him in shifting his customer base to ideal clients, he found that he needed to do the same for his coaching business. Choosing to work only with ideal clients makes a great deal of common sense but, once again, it isn't easy, especially if you feel you don't have enough clients. However, this single concept could vastly change the nature of business as we know it. The coach learned its value while working with Bob.

Finally, the coach learned that he can be very effective at and comfortable with helping others to make more money than he has ever made in his life and probably ever will.

A Final Most Important Lesson

As mentioned earlier, Bob and his coach began with two months of coaching, which the coach provided free of charge in order to gain coaching experience. Bob was the coach's first client. During this limited coaching period, it became clear that given Bob's desire for greater life balance, he would greatly benefit from a longer and more structured program. Bob's coach suggested such a program, one that would take roughly a year to complete. Afterward, the coach felt uncomfortable with that conversation, questioning whether his suggestion had come across as "salesy" and might be perceived as an attempt to shift Bob from a two-month free arrangement into a year-long paid coaching assignment. The coach felt very strongly that this program would benefit Bob whether he was Bob's coach or not, but he wasn't convinced that he had conveyed this well. At the suggestion of his own coach, he called Bob back the following day and shared his thoughts. Bob said he also had felt uncomfortable for the very reasons the coach had suspected, but by the end of their five-minute conversation he was convinced of the coach's sincerity and said that he would like to begin the program, on a paid basis, the following week.

This incident illustrates another simple, but not easy, lesson: Always speak the truth. If you are having a conversation on the inside that is inconsistent with the conversation you are having on the outside, part of the truth is missing. The essence of coaching is creating and supporting conversation that is absolutely honest and unconditionally constructive. There is no more important lesson: Be honest with yourself and others and live a truthful life. Living a truthful life will always keep you aligned with your values.

Questions for Discussion

1. When should a coaching relationship end?
2. How much structure is appropriate in a coaching relationship?
3. How do you measure the impact or ROI of achieving life balance and living a life of purpose and meaning?
4. What are the critical success factors for a successful coaching relationship?
5. What are the differences and similarities between a small business owner and a corporate executive? How would these differences alter, if at all, the nature of the coaching partnership?

The Author

Douglas A. Leland is a certified executive and business coach with more than 1,500 hours of one-on-one coaching experience. After five years as an officer in the U.S. Navy, he entered the health-care field as an operations manager. During his 20 years in health care, he served in staff and line positions, with the last 10 years in executive-level marketing and product development positions. He has senior staff and board of director experience in both for-profit and not-for-profit environments.

Leland has been a professional coach since 1998. He is a graduate of CoachU, a member of the International Coach Federation, and past board member of the San Diego Chapter of the Professional Coaches and Mentors Association. He is a graduate of the United States Naval Academy and Northeastern University's Executive MBA Program.

Leland lives in Coronado, California, with Sally, his wife of 28 years. They have two children, Heather and Zach, who are grown and creating their own lives. He can be reached at SOAR Worldwide, 420 C Avenue, Coronado, CA 92118; phone: 619.435.4660; email: doug@SOARworldwide.com.

Coaching in
a Clash of Culture

Trilogy Scientific

William Slebos

A newly hired director of a research and development (R&D) function, whose career had been spent in academia, was having trouble fitting in at Trilogy Scientific, a global corporation. Initially only recommended by the client's superiors, coaching was eventually required. The coaching was designed to be pragmatic, focusing on specific behaviors around specific interactions to increase the client's effectiveness as a corporate executive and as a leader of the entity for which he was responsible. After surviving the threat of termination, the client became a vice president in the corporation.

Organizational Profile

Headquartered in western Europe with major sites in North America and Europe, Trilogy Scientific conducts basic and applied scientific research relating to the impact of scientific advancement on the human condition. The company focuses on three major endeavors. First, it does theoretical predictive research to identify trends in science and specific anticipated achievements. Second, it purchases or licenses those achievements in their early states of development. Third, it develops those products for specific market applications and delivers them to the marketplace. Trilogy has 22,000 employees worldwide, has been in business in a variety of forms for 75 years, and is listed on the New York Stock Exchange.

This case was prepared to serve as a basis for discussion rather than to illustrate either effective or ineffective administrative and management practices. Names of places, organizations, or people have been disguised at the request of the author or organization.

Background

Michael, a European physician in his late forties, was hired by Trilogy as a director of an R&D function because he was internationally renowned as the developer of a scientific technique the company wanted to own and employ. This appointment was his first foray into the corporate world, having spent his entire career in academia, the last several years as the leader of an academic research enterprise with potentially profound industrial applications.

Many of Michael's behaviors, although acceptable in an academic environment, were not serving him well in the corporate world. He was offered coaching as a way of ameliorating the problems. Initially, Michael did not utilize the coaching. He was unaccustomed to having many of the services provided by the company's HR office, including coaching as a managerial tool. He felt the coaching was being forced on him. He had been enormously successful to this point in his career and saw no particular need to change anything, other than to try harder at what he was already doing. He was somewhat like a traveler in a foreign country who, not speaking the language, tries to be understood by speaking his or her native tongue more loudly and more slowly.

Several weeks later Michael was given 90-day notice that he would be released if his behaviors didn't change. Michael was then directed by the vice president to whom he reported to get coaching to help him integrate better into the culture of the company and to moderate or eliminate some of his behaviors that were creating obstacles to his effectiveness.

Michael's vice president, Carla, was a North American physician in her mid-forties. She was impatient with his habits and with the pace of his development and integration. Carla's department was gaining resources and responsibilities and a reputation for being a tough but professionally rewarding place to work. She did not appreciate the cultural differences Michael brought to the department and was publicly critical of some of them (for example, Michael's tardiness and his seeming disregard for policies and procedures—practices common in the academic world from which he had come). Michael made this gulf wider by blaming some of his shortcomings on those cultural differences.

In addition, members of Michael's leadership team were frustrated by his inattention at meetings, his tardiness, and his seeming unwillingness to give thorough consideration to their ideas.

Strategy

It is critical to understand what a successful coaching relationship is before discussing the strategy that begins the process. A useful definition of a coaching relationship is that it is a partnership based in trust and honesty that:

- focuses on issues and goals identified by the client
- encourages self-discovery on the part of the client
- challenges the client to acknowledge and exercise strengths and to recognize and modify or eliminate shortcomings.

Coaching is and should be intensely personal for both coach and client. When successful, it reaches a depth of intimacy and honesty in which the client speaks about personal issues that he or she knew at some level but was unable to articulate or validate. Perhaps the client was afraid or self-effacing, arrogant or uninformed. The central tenet is that the client holds both the knowledge regarding the problems in question and the answers to solve them. The role of the coach is to facilitate discovery and to tie together seemingly disparate events, thoughts, or behaviors. The challenge, and the thrill, for the coach is to see and expose the illusive.

In order for the coaching process to be meaningful for Michael, it had to be pragmatic and focused on specific behaviors involving specific interactions. This approach was driven by the threat of termination and by the fact that it was the method to which Michael could most readily relate and later employ. One of the conditions of the coaching agreement was that the coaching conversations would remain confidential and that any inquiries as to the progress of the coaching would be referred to Michael. Carla would measure his progress on bases other than the assessment of the coach. This agreement was acknowledged and honored by both the vice president and the HR staff. The fees for the coaching were paid from Michael's budget. The entire process was and continues to be conducted based on verbal agreements between Michael and the coach.

The Coaching Conversation
Starting Point

The initial task was to create a coaching relationship with Michael. Much of the first several sessions, which were done both in person and by telephone, involved Michael "painting a picture" of his professional and personal life. The conversations then led to his making assessments about his relative success and lack thereof in fitting into the company and his management of his staff and function. A good deal of time was spent in grounding and clarifying those assessments. The approach was and remains relatively simple. The coach asked Michael a series of questions similar to the following:

- What does the environment look like?
- What is working well for you?
- What is not working well for you?
- What do you want?
- Are there other ways to look at the environment?
- What are you going to do?

Access Point

Michael believed that what he was doing was in the best interests of the company, of his subordinates, and of the advancement of the science. He found the criticism of his actions confusing. He was used to operating as an independent agent and bridled at being closely managed. He felt that he was regularly upbraided for matters he deemed insignificant in the face of the progress being made in the scientific endeavor.

Much of the early coaching revolved around organizational culture, with Michael describing what the cultural expectations had been in the academic environment in which he had last worked. He needed to create a new set of behaviors for the corporate world in which he now found himself. Many of the coaching sessions were serendipitous and unscheduled, prompted by a meeting or decision that had presented itself in the fast-paced company. Michael started to understand that his success rested on his ability to position himself differently, to observe his environment in new ways, and in doing so to act in ways that first would do no harm and eventually would lead to the outcomes he sought. It was in these discussions that Michael began to formulate a new perception of his primary roles: to open doors for his staff both inside and outside the organization, to provide resources, to manage the performance of his staff, to provide forums in which the work of the department and its people could be heralded, and to be a good teammate. He continued to operate in his role as scientific leader and spokesperson.

After two months of individual coaching sessions, several events were held with the scientific leadership team, during which a set of operating norms was developed that addressed many of the behaviors both Michael and the staff identified as "getting in the way." Current work was discussed and short- and long-range planning was undertaken.

Following these events, members of Michael's leadership team continued to be interviewed by the coach on a regular basis to assess progress.

Point of Action

Within several months Michael found himself listening more, taking a broader view of the impact of his actions and of those around him, and anticipating obstacles and dealing with them more expeditiously. He began listening more to his staff and entrusting them with critical responsibilities. He recognized the absolute necessity of managing his relationship with his vice president and did so with aplomb. He learned that being right did not guarantee success, and he began to demonstrate his mastery of the fine art of timing.

Point of Celebration

It would be delightful to report that all went brilliantly as the coaching progressed. However, six months into the coaching process, Michael's performance review focused significantly on his early shortcomings, although it acknowledged his changes and growth. His increased compensation was accordingly modest. Michael was hurt, insulted, and discouraged. He thought he had made great strides, which in fact he had. At that point the coaching went to a much deeper level, delving into the meanings and interrelationship of life and work, the importance of recognition, trust, and truth. These were dark and difficult times for Michael. A good deal of the coaching time was spent exploring and affirming Michael's belief in himself.

Since his work remained fulfilling and scientifically important, Michael persisted. With coaching assistance, he built his team and expanded his business. He garnered greater resources in a shrinking environment. He refined the processes by which the work was done. He nurtured his internal and external partnerships and managed his vice president. When Carla left the company, Michael was promoted to vice president.

Measuring Success

As vice president within the R&D function, Michael has led his organization into areas of research and data collection unparalleled in his industry. He remains pleased with the coaching relationship and uses coaching in integrating new staff and regularly remaking his team. Today, he is an accomplished corporate executive and research scientist.

Lessons Learned

One of the key lessons has to do with the depth of the commitment and conversation often called for on the part of the coach. If coaches are going to encourage their clients to challenge the very place they occupy in the world, as they must, then coaches must be willing to do that as well. Coaches must admit that their "take" on the world is limited by their experiences and is narrow and biased no matter how hard they try to convince themselves otherwise.

Questions for Discussion

1. In what ways (for example, timing, breadth, or focus) might the coaching have been used differently to assist with the integration of the client?
2. What more concrete measures of success might have been used?
3. What sort of problems might a coach anticipate from a "forced" coaching situation?
4. What are the dangers for the coach in a situation in which the client's superior demands progress reports from the coach?
5. When is the coaching over?

The Author

William Slebos has been coaching people to do one thing or another since he was 13 years old. He has more than 30 years of experience in consulting with leaders in identifying current issues, facilitating change processes, and helping individuals and groups interact and perform more effectively. Particular areas of focus for Slebos' work involve coaching leaders and teams in dealing with particularly difficult or sensitive situations and intervening with organizations in crisis. Much of his work has been centered on the building and rebuilding of teams and helping his clients simplify and clarify their managerial lives and the impact of work on their personal lives. Slebos is a graduate of the University of North Carolina at Chapel Hill and spent 26 years working at Duke University. He is now owner and lead consultant of the Constellation Group, Durham, North Carolina, and is an affiliate of the Pyramid Resource Group. Slebos can be reached by phone at 919.620.7749 or by email at wslebos@mindspring.com.

The Coaching Zone

International Telecommunications Organization

Maureen Garrison and Geri England

A coaching initiative came to the forefront of this organization when the human resources organization development (HR OD) consultants realized that distinctions had been lost at the management team customer service level regarding the roles of leading, managing, and coaching. It was apparent that emphasis needed to be placed on coaching skills in order to manage the large teams resulting from process reengineering. As a result of these findings, the HR OD team recommended that the company's Culture Council place special emphasis on developing a strategic cultural initiative entitled The Coaching Zone. This now-trademarked initiative would provide an action-learning forum to instill coaching concepts, provide skills practice, and identify a customized deployment plan for the various regions and business channels across the country.

Organizational Profile

The telecommunications company had started as a rural telephone exchange in 1918. At the time of this coaching initiative, it had grown to be the fourth largest publicly owned telecommunications company serving retail and wholesale local exchange customers in franchise. The company had approximately 55,000 employees and provided local voice, video, and data services through approximately 22 million access lines. Its revenue stream in 1997 was approximately $14.6 billion dollars, an increase of more than $940 million from the previous year. For most of its existence, this company had functioned in

This case was prepared to serve as a basis for discussion rather than to illustrate either effective or ineffective administrative and management practices. Names of places, organizations, or people have been disguised at the request of the author or organization.

a regulated monopolistic environment that had created a paternalistic culture with a management style that directed and controlled instead of empowered and coached. The company was risk-averse and focused on solving problems instead of capitalizing on strengths.

The company valued its customers but, as a monopoly, was driven more by market forces. By mid-1995 the external business environment in which it operated had grown decidedly unfriendly. The company had weathered major reorganization, a substantial merger, process reengineering, and significant downsizing. The industry was anticipating dramatic changes to result from broad national legislation that was on the verge of congressional passage, while rising customer expectations were squeezing an already pressured industry. Every indicator pointed to a future of change, and those were just the external forces.

Inside the company, employees were feeling more and more disenfranchised as a result of the downsizing. Cost efficiency concerns were putting additional pressure on the company's employees, and the company was trying to devolve authority to the front line, remove management levels, increase speed to market, and change its employee/employer social contract. As a result, all employees, regardless of level, were feeling the effects of massive change with no end in sight. The company's senior leadership was becoming increasingly aware that opportunity and risk ran parallel in the newly competitive, highly technical world in which it now operated. Aware that the market opportunities could only be realized with a fully committed workforce, this team saw the need to hone its leadership capabilities and to design a plan to engage the frontline employees. The Coaching Zone initiative was designed as one of five strategic initiatives to assist at the frontline customer service level.

Background

The purpose of The Coaching Zone is to educate the company's management team in guiding (not telling) others to discover the best way to accomplish a goal. It also creates the distinction that coaching by managers is a creative partnership between a manager and his or her associates. This partnership allows the coach to connect with and inspire another to deliver his or her best performance at work while both parties are learning and growing personally and professionally. The organization needed to shift the view of coaching as a punitive intervention to one of guiding others toward a goal or accomplishment and asking them for their best. While they are working in the coaching zone, coaches are responsible for creating awareness of their client company's commitments and how they drive its workforce, challenging employees to become more self aware and knowledgeable, inspiring others to achieve stretch goals, preparing employees to use critical thinking skills, and helping them tap their internal wisdom in order to take appropriate actions.

The Coaching Zone workshop truly presented a new dimension of coaching that shifted coaching from a disciplinary tool to an empowering way of interacting with employees. It offered clear distinctions among various managerial roles and offered opportunities to apply the coaching skills learned in the workshop to real-world situations. After implementation of The Coaching Zone, employee opinion survey data indicated a positive trend in employee perceptions of the effectiveness of their supervisors' coaching. Over a six-month period the employee opinions of the managers who had acquired coaching skills were more positive by 10 points than the overall company average for managers.

The Coaching Zone Program

The Coaching Zone workshop consisted of one and one-half full days of training and coaching. It was designed to help managers attain their business results by more effectively coaching their employees. It provided an action-learning forum to instill coaching concepts, offered skills practice, and identified a customized deployment plan for 10 geographic regions and three business channels involving 26 states and 60,000 employees. The purpose of the workshop was to transfer key coaching skills, concepts, and models to midlevel managers and first-line coaches to create a new dynamic mindset around coaching. The Coaching Zone workshop introduced coaching concepts and skills; clarified distinctions for leading, managing, and coaching; and offered the opportunity to practice, practice, practice by bringing real-world coachable moments from the workplace into the sessions. During 1999, the audience for the workshop included senior leadership and their frontline direct reports who served the customers. Other participants included champions from the regions and business channels who were responsible for rolling out coaching workshops in their respective organizations. Figure 1 illustrates the demographics of workshop attendees.

Objectives for workshop participants included conducting an upfront self-assessment of coaching skills; understanding and practicing key coaching skills to enable their teams to accomplish their business

Figure 1. Demographics of Coaching Zone attendees.

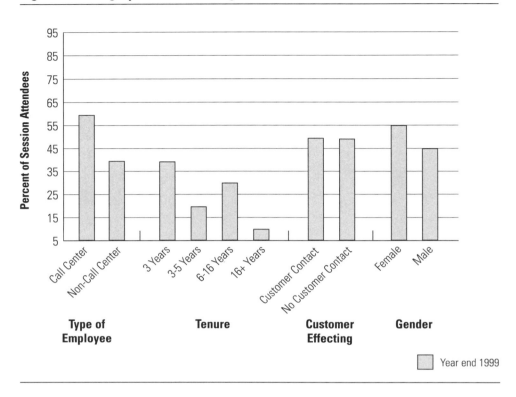

results; learning how to integrate appreciative inquiry, breakthrough thinking, and action learning into everyday coaching; modeling positive visible coaching behaviors to maintain or enhance results; and creating a personal action plan for coaching direct reports. There was also a request to tie the proposed action plans to specific company employee survey measures and to track results.

What Is Coaching?

Coaching within this organization is an interdevelopmental partnership with the primary focus on supporting employees in their professional development as well as their personal lives. Through a series of simple and consistent conversations, the coach and employee deepen their learning, leading to improved performance and enriched quality of life.

Coaching creates the optimum environment for coachable moments by using language and listening skills that allow the coach to fully focus on the person being coached. As it improves the ability to build relationships and make use of the people side of the business to achieve business results, coaching instills a climate in which employees achieve greater results in their performance, learning capabilities, and teaming attributes.

Coaching Process

The Coaching Zone was designed to shift the thinking of managers about their roles in developing their employees and how to best achieve the company objectives. This required a new mindset that moved from driving for results through any means to focusing on achieving results by developing and empowering employees. It helped managers clearly understand the differences between their coaching roles and their other roles. The Coaching Zone instilled new skills for interacting with employees in a holistic way so employees would take more accountability and responsibility for their decision making, their actions, and their own development.

At the center of The Coaching Zone is a model that has five key components—story, truth, source, shift, and solution—as well as five language and listening skills. These are generous listening, straight talk, powerful questions, effective requests, and action. Being in the Coaching Zone means operating throughout the model by using these newly acquired listening and language skills. Within the core model, a coach identifies the truth behind the story, gets to the source, and assists the employee in creating a shift in thinking that leads the employee toward a solution. It allows a coach to work with employees to truly identify what is behind the superficial conversation between them and assist employees to create a solution based on their internal wisdom and knowledge.

The Coaching Zone: Core Model

The following elaborates on the critical elements of The Coaching Zone's Core Model:

- *Story.* It's easy for a coach to get caught up in the story, but it is critical for the coach to find a way to detach from the story and move to what's behind it and identify the source of the problem.
- *Truth.* Truth is calling it as one sees it, and not being attached to the call if it isn't right. Sharing intuition regarding the truth allows

the employee to test the assumption and begin to assess what is really creating the need for coaching.

- *Source.* The source of any issue or problem is about the person in some way, not just the activity. Getting to the source provides the opportunity to see how that conversation is affecting the employee or peer and to speak to him or her about the underlying cause of the situation, not just the situation itself. Once the source is uncovered, the coach has created the possibility for the employee to shift to another perspective.
- *Shift.* By drawing attention to the gap between what is and what could be, the coach creates a change in the employee's perspective. The coach notices and labels where the employee is and the possibilities he or she sees for that individual.
- *Solutions.* Once the sources are uncovered, the coach's job is to look for and address authentic action, action that is designed to eliminate the problem as opposed to merely "handling it."

Best Practices

During the introductory segment of the workshop, participants are invited into a safe, confidential environment in which appreciative inquiry feedback tools and concepts are shared and seen as an essential part of learning. Appreciative Inquiry is a form of organizational study that actively seeks out and highlights times when people are at their best. Using this technique honors what each employee does well and does not make anyone feel he or she is wrong.

To familiarize participants with this appreciative concept, the coaches made the following points: When organizations are at their best, people at all levels of the organization engage in coaching with one another. Coaching for potential empowers people by showing them when they are on the right track and allows them freedom and encourages them to think for themselves. Such coaching helps people discover their own abilities. With the support that positive coaching provides, people find they can do amazing things. The coaches then asked for personal experiences: Describe a time when you coached someone successfully to do something challenging. What did you do? What did that feel like? What did you learn? In what areas would you like to do more coaching?

At the conclusion of the workshop, participants felt they needed structures to reinforce and sustain the coaching skills. Buddy coaches were assigned to coach and provide feedback and ongoing support to each other. Back at the workplace, coaching situations were discussed at regular staff meetings and practice sessions were held to reinforce the coaching skills.

Contracts and Code of Conduct for Coaching

The Coaching Zone introduced a code of ethics for coaches as well as a contract for coaching. The Coaching Zone Code of Ethics states in part:

> I acknowledge and honor a standard of high integrity, doing what is right for the employee, for the company, and for myself. I pledge to conduct myself responsibly, following a code of conduct that I establish as a foundation for my work as a coach. I also will communicate these standards with each employee and/or client.

Because the word "coaching" can have many definitions in an organization, The Coaching Zone Code of Conduct describes coaching as an active partnership that supports internal clients and employees in their professional development as well as their personal lives. In each coaching session, the employee and coach work together to choose the focus of the conversation. Before helping the employee to arrive at solutions, the coach listens, offers observations, and appreciatively questions the employee to uncover the source of any problem. This interaction creates clarity and moves the employee toward the appropriate action.

Specific standards of conduct that support this definition range from treating employees as adults to being a role model and communicating clearly how often the coaching sessions will be conducted. Coaches also will talk straight, maintain their roles as committed partners, and comply with company policies and procedures.

Integrating the Coaching Zone as a Strategic Cultural Initiative

Integrating coaching as a cultural initiative would align coaching as a needed skill within the organization and serve the Culture Council's mission, which was to:

> Provide the tools and support to build a knowledgeable, passionate, connected frontline team that wins in the marketplace. Each initiative has to be real, doable, sustainable, and frontline focused.

To strategically position coaching as a key element in the company's culture going forward, the HR OD team developed a multiphased process for presenting the program and obtaining approval from the Culture Council. The presentation outlined the premise, deployment, and implementation strategy for the program. To ensure consistency and linkage to the employee opinion survey data, a new question regarding coaching effectiveness was included in the survey.

Overall Strategic Design
Phase One: Coaching Zone Pilot Preparation

The first stage included program development and coaching training of the HR OD team. It was at this point that the internal HR OD consultants quickly realized they were not fully equipped to develop, design, and lead coaching workshops within the company. They developed a comprehensive request-for-proposal and sent this to five external coaching firms. This process identified the Pyramid Resource Group as a full-service coaching consortium that would assist in development of the internal HR OD practitioner's skill sets and begin the codevelopment of a pilot workshop.

Phase Two: Conduct Coaching Zone Pilot

The Pyramid Resource Group conducted the pilot in May 1999. This two-day workshop provided an action-learning forum to instill coaching concepts, provide skills practice, and identify a customized deployment plan for various regions and business channels. At the outset of the program, participants felt that "leadership" needed to be at the session and that coaching is something we "do to others." They wanted to learn how to coach others, not to be coached themselves. Participants learned in the workshop that shifting to a "culture of coaching" would lead to reaching the numbers, but that focusing on the numbers creates fear and causes employees to burn out. The culture shift needed to include development and performance, balancing work/life issues, communicating upward more effectively, and energizing employees while improving performance. The participants left the workshop committed to creating this culture of coaching.

Once the workshop concluded, attendees provided feedback on the workshop contents, made suggestions to strengthen the content, and agreed on a deployment strategy for the entire company. Feedback received during the pilot positively highlighted the use of actual coaching experiences from the field, practice in listening and straight-talk skills, the use of appreciative inquiry, and the effective placement of video segments throughout the program.

Attendee comments included the following:
- "Coaching skills training is desperately needed at all management levels."
- "Union and management agreed that increasing frontline coaching skills is key to obtaining frontline buy-in to new union/management partnership initiative."

- "Effective coaching skills learned during this workshop will have the ability to reinforce new behaviors of our new management/union partnership."
- "There are many first- and second-line coaches that are new to the industry. We face a situation where we have coaches . . . who need help not only in strengthening their coaching skills but are also looking for, and need mentoring from, someone who knows how the business works."
- "Having come here from the outside, I think there is a lot of room for improvement in this area."
- "Leaders have to set the stage for the midlevel management team to be successful. Leaders need to acquire skills at the outset to ensure next-level success."

Phase Three: Post-Pilot Activity

With the Culture Council's approval and senior leadership's funding, the implementation of this strategy was approved and a deployment schedule identified. The primary intent of this new approach was to provide a forum in which frontline managers could learn new skills and begin to integrate coaching principles and skills into day-to-day coaching conversations. Once this process had begun, the HR OD team would shift its focus to ensuring that coaching skills and competencies were aligned with HR policies and procedures, and performance measurement goals.

Target Measures and Measuring Success

As measures of the coaching initiative, the Culture Council selected three employee opinion survey questions that would measure areas the council wanted to positively maintain or improve. The supervisor question is depicted in figure 2. The data compares the scores of departments that implemented the coaching workshops (departments 1 and 2) with one department that passed on the opportunity to deploy this initiative (department 3) and the overall company average. As the figure shows, the positive responses from the two departments using the workshops were consistently higher than those from the company as a whole or the department that passed up the workshops.

Point of Celebration

To continue to embrace appreciative inquiry as a tool within the context of coaching, the HR OD consultants launched a program called

Figure 2. Question one of employee opinion survey.

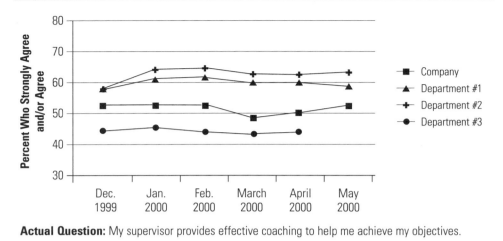

Actual Question: My supervisor provides effective coaching to help me achieve my objectives.

An Appreciative Study of Coaching across eight of the organization's customer service call centers. Seventy-nine management, hourly, and union employees participated as interviewers, conducting 460 interviews regarding participants' experiences with being coached or coaching others. Positive responses from these interviews included the value of the following:
• helping others discover for themselves the answers they already had
• seeing the best in each employee
• generalizing the lessons from one person's success to the entire center
• seeing others grow their own successes
• meeting the challenge of guiding others toward their potential
• creating the strong bond that results from a coaching partnership.
    What employees valued the most from their coaching experiences were
• having a voice and being heard
• honesty (straight talk) regarding job performance strengths and weaknesses
• sincerity
• expressions of confidence in their abilities
• a coach who would truly stop what he or she was doing and listen
• recognition of their years of experience on the job.
    After this experience, the participants worked together during a two-day summit meeting to create a possibility statement for coaching that stated:

Our company is an exciting place to work; all team members are empowered and involved in identifying needs and implementing action. Encouragement makes it happen. Recognition makes it a habit.

Measuring Success
Benchmarking

To ensure that the company would be able to benchmark itself against best-in-class companies, the HR OD consultants contacted their counterparts within companies that were members of the Mayflower Consortium and requested their assistance in identifying performance coaching questions. Mayflower is a consortium of *Fortune* 500 companies whose members benchmark against each other using a group of "core" employee opinion survey questions. Other benefits of this membership include the ability to network with other organizations and learn from them, and to find answers to key questions regarding employee strategies. The HR OD team reviewed several coaching for performance questions, such as the one shown in figure 2, and incorporated these into the company's monthly employee opinion poll.

Coaching Zone Workshop Results

Between 1999 and 2000, HR conducted 60 one-and-one-half-day Coaching Zone workshops focusing on real-world practice and application of skills. As figure 3 shows, the 1,300 attendees gave the workshop an overall quality rating of 98.7.

Employee Opinion Survey Results

Additional employee opinion survey results were also being tracked for the Culture Council's five overall strategic culture initiatives (one

Figure 3. Results of Coaching Zone workshops.

1999-2000 Numbers	Participant Feedback
• Three internal OD team	• This is the missing link to our process reengineering efforts.
• Six external coaches	• Even if we do this badly, it's better than what we have now.
• 60 1.5-day sessions	• Finally, a workshop where I can immediately apply what I learned.
• 1,300 participants	
— middle management	
— frontline coaches	
• Overall quality rating	
— 98.7% excellent	

of which was the coaching initiative). The improved results, shown in figure 4, support how well the Culture Council remained true to its mission of providing the tools and resources necessary to create a passionate, connected, and knowledgeable frontline workforce that would win in the marketplace.

Changes Based on Workshops and Surveys

Employees all have their own talents and skills, desires for success, and dreams. The coach's job is to give them access to those abilities and dreams and to help them discover their most powerful and productive aspects as coaching takes place during a series of conversations.

Figure 4. Employee opinion survey results.

	Favorable Responses			
Questions	**1995**	**1997**	**1998**	**1999– May 2000**
I **feel encouraged** to come up with new and better ways of doing things.	23%	36%	42%	45/47%
How would you rate the organization as a company **to work for**?	30%	45%	48%	47/47%
Considering everything, how would you rate your **overall satisfaction** at this time?	28%	50%	55%	53/55%
I have the freedom **to make decisions to** get the job done.	35%	46%	51%	47/50%
How satisfied are you with the **recognition** received for doing a good job?	23%	32%	40%	49/46%

Participant Reaction/Feedback:
- "I was able to relate to and actually take something back. All other classes would end in 'But how am I going to use this?' I have been with this company for two years and I have attended three coaching classes. This is the first workshop where I have learned skills and concepts that I feel I can do. Thanks."

- "I would like to see a follow-up, a commitment to continue this program in all areas of business."

- "I have a new understanding about the fact that coaching is all about the employee. I feel that this is a wonderful new approach to coaching that I will definitely try."

- "For once we were able to receive practice and retain the tools and instruction needed in an acceptable amount of time."

Coaching is a profound commitment to the growth and development of each individual employee.

The coaching and development competency definition needed to be aligned across the organization and include behavioral attributes that were in line with Coaching Zone skills and concepts. Developing a self-assessment guide to assess their competencies before attending a session allowed participants time to think about their strengths and weaknesses, ask the most productive questions during the workshop, and create a development plan targeted at actual coachable moments that they could immediately apply upon returning to work.

Future Coaching Zone workshops needed to include knowledge and skills transfer to midlevel management champions within the regions and the business lines, and collaboration between internal HR groups, HR OD consultants and coaching partners, and regional and business line champions to create customized designs for deployment. In addition, it was important to continue the development of the HR OD consultants as subject matter experts and coaching partners within the regions and business lines, strengthening their value and role in the organization.

Workshops needed to have various rollout options, which included customized workshops for regions and business lines and varying design options to meet the special requirements of each group. Other steps included integrating key skills into existing and new training courses and linkage to such initiatives as Coaches Clinics, Coaches Notes, and a Coaches Toolkit to ensure an integrated approach. These tools were necessary to ensure knowledge and skills transfer to midlevel management champions within the regions and the business lines.

Applying Knowledge, Insights, and Skills Gained through the Coaching Process

In the Coaching Zone, leaders don't always have the answers. They partner with employees to bring their best thinking to the table, a partnership we call The Quest. The coaching relationship is a creative search, a bold adventure of discovery, achievement, and fulfillment. It is a quest for high standards, breakthrough thinking, and concrete actions.

The beauty of the Coaching Zone is that everyone works more effectively and creatively when they are pulled toward what they want instead of being pushed toward it. The concept of "gap" is critical to coaching: When the coach helps an employee create the right gap between where the employee is and where he or she wants to be, motivation is automatic. The major shift in thinking for the management team was the ability to stop for a moment and ask, "How do I lead this quest when I don't have the answers myself?" This is a critical point: The coach is part of the quest and is not required to have all the answers. In coaching, the power comes from discovery on the part of both coach and the coached.

The manager and employee work together to agree on a gap that is important enough to warrant a coaching relationship. The role of a coach is to help the employee identify and bridge this gap. The manager listens generously and speaks straightforwardly. Now is the time for him or her to begin thinking. "What are the questions that need to be asked or the requests that need to be made to get the employee to find his or her own way to bridge the gap?"

The manager coach may have some answers, the employee may have some, and some may remain for both to discover together in their conversations. The coach has two primary language tools as strong partners in this quest: questions and requests. Both are forms of inquiry the coach uses as action tools. Powerful questions prompt employees to bring their best thinking to the table while requests prompt them to take action. For example, a powerful question would be "What would it take to reach that sales goal?" A request would evoke a response that would produce committed action on the employee's part: "Harold, will you start making 20 after-market sales calls every day for a month?"

To be a great coach, the managers learned that they must be committed to the development of each employee and his or her performance, not just committed to winning. The managers also learned that, to become great coaches, they had to become role models for all the qualities they expected from others, including self-care and a sense of work/life balance.

Return-on-Investment

Overall benefits achieved by implementing this coaching initiative included

- a standard coaching model throughout the participating organizations with consistency in coaching terminology at all levels and in all groups
- skilled midlevel managers who could act as coaches and champions for coaching throughout the participating business units and regions
- the development of internal HR OD consultants into highly skilled internal mentors and coaching partners who had the materials and skills needed for future coaching initiatives
- linkage to employee opinion survey measures and the development of self-assessment coaching skills tools

- internal video media to support the design of additional tools and resources and coaching skills training materials
- linkage to other frontline culture initiatives to ensure integration across the organization; for example, additional tools to foster better union/management relations
- a foundation for regional coaching forums to impart and reinforce the coaching concepts and allow skills practice.

Return-on-investment from a financial perspective is not available due to the company's merger with another large telecommunications corporation.

Lessons Learned
From a Corporate Perspective

Frontline managers and coaches within various departments (sales, customer service, and facilities) were required to achieve different sets of competencies. This insight provided the HR OD team with the opportunity to bring a cross-functional team of leaders together to assess this situation and move toward identifying a common set of frontline coaching competencies: quality focus, communication, customer focus, driving for results, interpersonal relations, and decision making and judgment.

It became apparent from the workshops that managers were enabling their employees to be dependent by giving them the answers instead of encouraging them to find their own answers. By placing emphasis on listening and questioning skills, participants were able to shift from offering solutions to helping others generate their own. Because many new managers did not understand basic psychology and human motivation, self-discovery exercises were incorporated in the workshops to help participants understand the sources of employee concerns and motivations.

A safe environment had to be created in the workshops to enable participants to share their real situations honestly.

Skill transfer came only through multiple practice coaching interactions using real-work situations and not role-playing activities.

The Coaching Zone had to be broadened to create a culture of coaching. This was accomplished by deploying coaching workshops across the organization and reinforcing key skills, concepts, and models by developing a CD-ROM-based e-learning refresher and a second session, Deepening the Learning, in which we could solicit 100 alumni of Phase One to test the workshop design. This was followed by modification and redeployment.

To ensure that coaching remained a part of the organization's culture, HR worked on the development of a Coaching Performance Model to include a coaching competency model, a 360-degree coaching tool, and continuing study of best practices. HR also began to integrate coaching into HR practices, including selection tools, performance management, training, compensation, rewards and recognition, succession planning, and career development.

Participant Insights

The biggest insight was learning about the power of the positive question: Asking the right questions empowered the coach and the employee, and questions became the keys to creative thinking. Coaches began to ask questions when they needed more information. They also asked questions when they wanted someone to think more creatively. They asked questions when they suspected someone might have the answer, and they always asked questions when an employee needed someone to listen.

A second insight was that the language used when asking questions needs to be simple. Fact-finding questions can be as simple as "Can you tell me more about that?" "What other things did you try?" or "Exactly what did he tell you?" Questions can also probe creatively by posing such inquiries as "If you had a magic wand, what would you do for the customer?" or "If you had an opportunity to interview the world's leading expert in this area, what do you think she or he would tell you to do?"

In the Coaching Zone, the coach could check for the obvious by asking, "Do you have an answer?" or "How can I help you with that?" Coaches began to feel comfortable with a culture in which they did not have to have all the answers all the time.

The next insight was related to David Cooperrider's Anticipatory Principle: Employees behave according to what they believe about the future. Encouraging employees to change their images of the future will in fact create a different future. Coaches learned that what they ask when coaching employees determines what the employee finds. What they find determines how they talk, how they talk determines what they imagine, and what they imagine determines what they achieve.

Leadership comments from those who attended the workshop included

- "Even if we [implement the Coaching Zone Workshop] badly, it's better than doing nothing at all."
- "This is the missing link between our process reengineering efforts and today. We should have done this five years ago."

Questions for Discussion

1. Leaders want a lot from others . . . a coach can also want a lot *for* others. Typically, the only thing that gets communicated frequently enough is what the manager wants from people. The focus needed to shift to communicating what the manager wants for people.

- What are the top five things you need and want from your employees or associates?
- List the top five things you want for all your employees or associates (a great life, a feeling of success—make it personal). Remove the generalities from what you just wrote, making it personal, honest, and big.

  Remember: Wanting more for your employees than they see for themselves gives them an idea of what is possible. As their coach, you're in the best position to see their talent and potential. Helping them to see these too helps them be their best.

2. Where do coaching competencies lie in your organization or in yourself? Are they aligned with your organization's performance management systems?

3. Where does actual coaching take place in your organization today (sales, performance)?

4. What is the perception of coaching in your organization?

5. What are the steps you need to take to create a culture of coaching?

The Authors

Maureen Garrison, having recently completed more than 20 years with the telecommunications company described in this chapter, is also a professional co-active coach certified through the Coaches' Training Institute. Garrison served as director of organization effectiveness, with responsibility for change management and culture change in support of 65,000 employees in 28 states. In this role, she was recognized for leading human performance, productivity, and cultural initiatives to achieve goals through people. She is active in the human resources profession and is currently a member of the International Coach Federation (ICF), American Society of Training & Development (ASTD), Organization Development Network, National Association of Female Executives, and the Institute for OD Professionals. In 1997 she was recognized by ASTD with an Excellence in Practice Award.

Garrison is a frequent presenter with a variety of audiences where she addresses coaching and change management strategies to benchmark companies. Her speaking engagements at professional conferences have included the International Quality & Productivity Conference in 1996, ASTD European Benchmarking Forum in 1998, the 1999 Institute for Workforce Development, and 1999 keynote presenter at the Fourth International Coach Federation Conference (ICF), with a follow-up presentation during the 2000 conference. She spoke at the First International Appreciative Inquiry Conference in 2001 in Baltimore, Maryland. In 2001, Garrison founded The Consulting Zone and now works as a consultant with corporations, creating new dimensions in navigating organizational change, group coaching, achieving breakthrough results, and creating new management/union partnerships. You can reach her at Maureen@theconsultingzone.com.

Geri England is a manager and coach in the workforce performance department of her organization. In her current role, she is responsible for coaching, change management and culture initiatives, training, and organizational development. She is also a professional co-active coach certified through the Coaches Training Institute and coaches individuals and teams in her organization. The focus of her work is on performance improvement through people-oriented strategies. Coaching, appreciative inquiry, creativity, and breakthrough thinking approaches have been cornerstones of designs she has customized for clients.

England was part of the team that won the ASTD Excellence in Practice Award for Change Initiatives in 1997, and she presented the case study at the ASTD Benchmarking Forum in 1998. Since 1986 she has led numerous training, organizational development, and coaching workshops and has presented to the International Career Management Association, ASTD, and the first International Appreciative Inquiry Conference in 2001. She is a member of the International Coach Federation and the American Society of Training & Development. She also is a volunteer ESL teacher for Spanish speakers in Dallas, Texas.

The Executive Coach as a Foreign Agent: How Stupid Questions Can Lead to Greatness

Manufacturing Company

John Renesch

This case study illustrates how an independent coach acted as a confidential sounding board for a leading executive and influenced the way he conducts business. Sometimes the loneliest positions in an organization can be at the very top. It might appear to most people in the lower ranks that the person in the highest position—where the most power is generally concentrated—has the most support and the greatest degree of attention, but the person standing in those shoes often feels very alone and isolated.

When someone rises to the higher ranks in any organization, there is a tendency to adopt a protective posture so that this cherished position—which was achieved through great effort, dedication, and often sacrifice over many years—can be securely maintained. Great pains are taken to protect one's position so that, although he or she might rise still higher in the existing organization or another one, the executive still might fear slipping backward and losing status, position, or compensation. In this protective mode, there is great reluctance to become very vulnerable with one's co-workers. After all, the executives think, "why give my competition any ammunition that they could use against me later?"

A private, independent coach is a confidential sounding board, an outside confidante who feels safe. Since the coach does not work with, socialize with, or even know the executive's co-workers, the executive feels more comfortable being authentic and relaxed—qualities that allow him or her to receive the maximum benefit from being coached.

This case was prepared to serve as a basis for discussion rather than to illustrate either effective or ineffective administrative and management practices. Names of places, organizations, or people have been disguised at the request of the author or organization.

Background

Rich is CEO and chairman of one of the largest manufacturing companies in his industry, with plants in more than 20 countries. His world-leading company's stock is widely held and publicly traded on the New York Stock Exchange. Rich founded the company more than 25 years ago and has been at the helm continuously, leading its IPO in the 1980s. As he contemplated his retirement and succession in the late 1990s, he started thinking about the legacy he'd leave and retained an executive coach to work with him on a highly confidential basis. He wanted someone who had been a CEO—someone who knew what it was like to be in his shoes. Initially, Rich wanted a coach who "knew the business," but fortunately, this didn't happen. Although he found a seasoned veteran executive he liked, the coach didn't know anything about his industry. The coach was a real "foreigner," but he did know what it was like to run an organization.

Finding the Right Coach

Rich read several business books each year, seeking out the most progressive titles and shunning the usual "top ten" management books to which most of his peers seemed to flock. He wasn't particularly interested in having the politically correct management books on display on his credenza or being fluent in the latest jargon or "flavor of the month" management fad. In particular, he appreciated books about learning organizations, systems thinking, personal development, chaos and complexity theory—all subjects that stretched his mind and challenged his thinking.

One particular writer—something of a business philosopher—kept showing up in Rich's stack of books to be read. He liked what this man wrote, as well as his straightforward style. After noticing the author's magazine articles, he subscribed to the author's monthly newsletter.

One day, quite spontaneously, Rich was so moved by one of this man's articles that he emailed the writer and asked if he was available for a private consultation. After a brief conversation, the two men agreed to have regular telephone calls that would provide Rich with a regular "touchstone" on a routine basis. Originally, they started at a frequency of twice a month but soon increased this to weekly.

Not knowing any of the "conventions" for the industry, or "the way things are done around here," Rich's coach asked him "stupid" questions—questions that pushed Rich to look beyond the ways he had done things for more than 20 years. Rich discovered that, in many ways, he had become a prisoner of his own know-how. What he had learned from his success had become a hindrance to moving forward. Through the process of inquiry initiated by his coach, Rich was soon seeing a number of options he had never before entertained.

As a result of his coaching experience, Rich committed himself and his company to a huge goal: to become an environmentally sustainable operation within four years. This meant that the company, which had manufacturing plants in more than 20 other countries and was a major polluter in all those environments, would have a net-zero impact on nature worldwide in just 48 months. As Rich led the organization toward this ambitious goal, it became an industry leader in another category: nature-friendly corporations. He eventually wrote a book about his self-described "epiphany." His extraordinary honesty resulted in his leaving an even greater legacy: a rare insight into the heart and soul of an enlightened business leader who has become an exemplar for sustainable business and corporate social responsibility. In addition to increasing profits and supporting a healthy value for its stock, his company is now one of the most admired corporations in the world for its pioneering efforts in "green business."

As do most leaders, Rich knew that he had the attention of everyone in the company. He knew he could snap his fingers and get a rapid response from direct reports, as well as anyone else lower on the corporate ladder. As did Rich, many leaders confuse this deferential treatment with actual support, both personal and organizational. Others recognize that people are often motivated by self-interest. Once executives become accustomed to this ingratiating treatment they can easily slip into believing that all of these people are really their friends and have their best interests at heart.

As in the boiled-frog parable—in which a frog won't notice until too late the slow increase of heat as the pot of water he occupies comes to a boil—slow and gradual change often goes unrecognized. This can be as true of executives as well as it can be of frogs. After the first five or six sessions with his coach, Rich began to realize how comfortable he had become in his little "fortress of familiarity," feeling almost cocky about his situation. Although it was somewhat shocking to his ego, he welcomed the straightforward feedback he was getting from his new coach. He also started noticing how restrained he had been in his thinking about his role as one of the key leaders in the organization. He started seeing how he had grown comfortable within very limited parameters defined by the corporate culture.

As did the naked emperor in the tale of The Emperor's New Clothes, the boss needs to get accurate and objective feedback if he or she is going to be as effective as possible in leading the organization toward its purpose and fulfilling its mission.

Being Open to "Foreign" Input

Organizations are systems made up of and run by people. In manufacturing, there are also mechanical systems involving equipment and material. But service organizations are, for the most part, purely human systems. Students of systems thinking quickly learn the difference between "open" and "closed" systems. Open systems allow input and feedback from outside of themselves; that is, input "foreign" to the system's own "party line." Closed systems tend to reject or repel any foreign input. When a system becomes closed, it becomes bureaucratic or dysfunctional, more focused on its own survival than in accomplishing its mission. Its first task is to repel anything deemed "foreign," much as the human body's immune system goes into action whenever an invading agent, such as a virus or infection, is detected.

After experiencing how reluctant he was at first to hear feedback offered by his coach, Rich could see how similar feedback given to the organization could be met with major resistance. He could appreciate how one person might take in the feedback and recognize the value in it, as he was doing, but that the whole system might collectively see the same feedback as threatening the status quo. Rich could tell that if he hadn't read so much and understood some things about how systems behaved before he retained his coach, he might have been far less open to the frank and honest feedback be received. He might have opted to remain in his comfort zone, "believing his own PR" as the heat under him slowly rose.

Systemantics, a little-known book published in 1990, takes a light-hearted look at how systems operate, which is often seen as a heavy, serious academic subject. The author, John Gall, suggests, "Any large system is going to be operating most of the time in failure mode." As difficult as this may be for most people to digest, experienced business leaders know that the more complex an organization becomes, the less likely it is to perform as efficiently as a small team of skilled people. On some level, most of us know that organizations are cumbersome and not particularly efficient.

Another piece of wisdom from *Systemantics:* "In a closed system, information tends to decrease and hallucination to increase." As any organization gets more bureaucratic and dysfunctional, it can foster a delusory hallucination that things aren't really as bad as they may seem.

The noted systems thinking expert Peter Senge once told me that any time you have a group of skilled people all working with good intentions but results that are not up to expectations, there's most likely a problem with the system, not the people. It is the fault of the system they are working in—the corporate culture, group core beliefs, conventions, time delays, communications, trust levels, and a variety of other factors that affect how people relate to each other within the larger system.

Leaders of these organizations—human systems—are usually not receiving objective input from the people who report to them: It is structurally impossible to achieve truly objective input from anyone who is embedded in the system. After all, everyone inside the system has a stake in it, has relationships with people in it, and probably ascribes to its tenets or "the way things are done around here." Even vendors who provide services to the company are part of the system after a short time of working with it. The only way to get objective input is from someone who is outside the system. The farther the input is from the heart of the system, and the newer it is, the more objective it will be.

Rich's coach was from outside his industry, and thus was far removed from the heart of his corporate system. So, in the early weeks of the relationship, the coach felt powerfully intuitive and willing to confront his client on difficult matters. After about four months of private coaching, however, the coach began to notice some uneasiness in his sessions with Rich. He paid particular attention to this feeling and, thanks to his extensive experience, started to realize that this uneasiness had to do with his own feelings of "co-optedness." He had started to feel protective about his contractual arrangement and was feeling restricted by many of the issues that had held back his client. He started thinking like Rich, agreeing with him. He liked working with Rich—a man of great insight, courage, and integrity. Feeling protective of this arrangement, he was less brave, a bit less bold in his Socratic probings. He started to feel some hesitancy in taking Rich on over tough issues. Once he realized this, the coach saw that he was in danger of losing some of his "outside the system" perspective.

With this realization, he knew that he either had to reclaim his external perspective or suggest that Rich find a new coach. Once he realized this, it was easier to revive his integrity and reclaim his objectivity. He continued to work with Rich, but he was now unattached to his role and remained willing to replace himself whenever he felt he was losing his detached perspective.

The Coach as a Foreign Agent

A professional executive coach has the potential to act as a "foreign agent." In fact, being external to the system gives the coach the right to ask questions that the CEO may never be asked by his or her subordinates because they're too "in the know" to ask such "silly" questions. But the external, private coach can be humbly spontaneous, and ask the obvious questions—questions that are obvious only to the outsider, the foreigner to the system.

Summary

If Rich hadn't gotten "foreign" input—feedback from a source far removed from his organization as well as his industry—he might never have discovered his current passion. His company might never have achieved its new reputation as an exemplar in a world growing increasingly concerned over the natural environment and the devastating impact much of business is having on the Earth. And, if Rich had gotten his way, he would have retained a coach who was not all that foreign to his business, which probably would not have resulted in such breakthrough results.

When coaching a leader, the results often cannot be easily measured in tangible terms, but the leader-client usually knows if the coaching sessions are valuable and can rank that value subjectively. In this case, Rich was extremely pleased with the work done. The company enjoyed a greatly enhanced public image, which resulted in articles and interviews and features on the company that money could not have bought. And, despite the initial investments the company made to achieve its goal of having a net-zero effect on the environment—what Rich called becoming a "sustainable company" within four years—its earnings never lagged sufficiently to directly affect its stock value.

The value of executive coaching is greatly enhanced by the coach being outside the conditions in which the client lives every day. As a "foreign agent," the coach can ask the stupid questions that allow for new perspectives to come to light for the client. This is real discovery—self-discovery—in which the client finds something that has been living inside, something the soul knows but the mind hasn't yet grasped. This is where passion is waiting to be born, and the executive coach can help the client bring this passion to the surface and become even more alive.

Lessons Learned

Some of the key lessons learned from this coaching experience are listed below.

- A question that might be obvious to anyone outside of the system might never be considered by those within it because the answer is assumed to be so obvious. For instance, how often do people inside an organization ask, "Why are we in business?" or "Why do we do what we do?"
- A naïve question from someone who is "outside" can provoke the most intense introspective process if it is valued by the receiver. For instance, many years ago the question "What business are we in?" prompted railroads to see that they were in the transportation industry, expanding their context significantly.
- Genuine creativity and innovation come from humility—seeing everything as if for the first time, like a child—and this usually comes out of a willingness to ask stupid questions.
- There is always something to learn; when people or organizations stop learning, they start dying. It is only a matter of time before they are dead.

Questions for Discussion

1. Are you willing to come across as naïve and perhaps "stupid" by asking what may seem like dumb questions?
2. How much do you trust your intuition when a question to ask your client presents itself?
3. What would you need to do in order to better trust your own intuition about this?
4. How will you know when you are becoming co-opted by the system—when your own agenda starts taking precedence over the interests of your client?
5. Are you able to replace yourself if you feel you are co-opted and you can't get free of it?
6. Can you confront your client on really tough issues and risk getting fired if he or she chooses to do so?

The Author

John Renesch is a San Francisco businessman with more than 30 years' experience as a chief executive, principal, and entrepreneur. He is now a business futurist, speaker, and writer. He is the author of numerous books, including *Learning Organizations and New Traditions in Business*. Leadership guru and author Warren Bennis calls Renesch "a wise elder who shines with wisdom." Stanford School of Business professor emeritus Michael Ray calls him "a beacon lighting the way to a new paradigm." *The Futurist* magazine calls him a "business visionary." His latest book is *Getting to the Better Future*. On a discreet and confidential basis, Renesch coaches senior business leaders. He can be reached at www.Renesch.com.

References

Gall, John. *Systemantics: The Underground Text of Systems Lore*. Ann Arbor: The General Systemantics Press, 1990.

Further Resources

Chawla, Sarita and John Renesch, editors. *Learning Organizations: Developing Cultures for Tomorrow's Workplace*. Portland, Oregon: Productivity Press, 1995.

Ferrucci, Piero. *Inevitable Grace: Breakthroughs in the Lives of Great Men and Women: Guides to Your Self-Realization*. New York: Tarcher/Putnam, 1990.

Harman, Willis. *Global Mind Change*. San Francisco: Berrett-Koehler, 1998.

O'Neil, John. *The Paradox of Success*. New York: Tarcher/Putnam, 1994.

How Sandy Got Her Groove Back

KBY Financial Services

Kathy Baske Young

This story showcases the value of executive coaching to a newly-promoted vice president of sales for an international finance company, whose self-confidence and feelings of self-worth were being decimated by a nonsupportive boss.

Although she was also a wife and mother, she defined herself by her job to a large extent. A recent promotion into a new area of responsibility, coupled with a lack of acknowledgement of her achievements at work and her boss's critical management style, had turned a bright, successful, confident professional into an insecure person filled with self-doubt.

The client came to coaching to sort through such issues as whether she was in over her head, why her past success strategies weren't working, how she should manage her boss, and how she could deal with the overwhelming insecurity that was affecting both her work and personal lives.

Coaching Sandy involved helping her see her situation from a different perspective, enabling her to step back from the day-to-day details and look at her progress on a continuum. It looked at the areas in which she felt most vulnerable and enabled her to design a work scenario and make some confident strategic career decisions.

Organizational Profile and Background

KBY Financial Services is an international company headquartered on the East Coast. Its product line includes investment services, mortgages, credit cards, and other related financial services. Sandy is an over-achiever who had always excelled in everything she had

This case was prepared to serve as a basis for discussion rather than to illustrate either effective or ineffective administrative and management practices. Names of places, organizations, or people have been disguised at the request of the author or organization.

taken on—until now. She had been promoted to vice president of domestic sales for one of the largest product lines of an international financial services company, despite her lack of direct sales experience. In that role, she was responsible for a billion dollars of revenue and multiple product lines. She had always been a star performer, rising quickly through the ranks of the companies where she worked.

Now, one year into the new position, she was a wreck. She had lost her confidence, was getting no positive feedback from her boss, and was working an increasing number of hours in an attempt to turn around the situation she had inherited. While the feedback and performance from her staff seemed to indicate a positive trend, she was not getting the same feedback from her boss.

Sandy was referred to coaching through the HR department, as one of several executives it was referring to an executive coach. HR staff was aware of her frustration since she had taken on her new position and they were concerned about the hours she was putting in and some performance comments from her boss. Sandy had always been an upbeat and positive star performer. The HR staff wanted her to have support outside the company so she felt safe talking about what was going on. In fact, Sandy was resistant to asking for any kind of help because she had always been so self-sufficient and proud.

Sandy agreed to work with a coach because she wanted to succeed in the new position and was starting to wonder if her lack of sales experience was a barrier to her success in this role. She wanted the coach to help her get back on track, so she could once again get the outstanding reviews and success she had long enjoyed. She did feel that her coach's background in sales management might be helpful to her, but she was reluctant to share her feelings of inadequacies with her coach—a total stranger—at the beginning.

Sandy felt she was walking a tightrope because every change she made was interpreted as a reflection on the problems she inherited from her boss, who had held the job before her. She felt as if she was damned if she made changes and damned if she didn't. She needed her coach to help her see what she couldn't see, because she wanted to keep the job and be successful.

Strategy

Professional coaches provide an ongoing partnership designed to help clients produce fulfilling results in their personal and professional lives. Coaches help people improve their performance and enhance the quality of their lives.

Coaches are trained to listen, to observe, and to customize their approach to individual client needs. They seek to elicit solutions and strategies from their clients; they believe the client is naturally creative and resourceful. The coach's job is to provide support that will enhance the skills, resources, and creativity that the client already has.

It was important that the coach listen deeply to what was going on with Sandy and ask the right questions. Was this a situation in which her talents didn't match the demands of the job? If so, let's call it and move on. Was this a situation in which she was doing the right things, but something else was going on? Was her stress about how she performed or how she thought others viewed her performance? What strategies had been successful in the past? Why weren't they working in her new position?

On a personal level, the coach needed to find out what this was doing to her family and her health, what was at stake beyond the job, why she was willing to put herself through this, and what was really important to her.

She worked seven days most weeks, traveled fairly often, and was the primary wage-earner. Her days were long and intense. She felt the weight of the financial burden on her shoulders: She had three small children at home. Although there was obviously a financial need to succeed, there was something more to it: With her track record for the previous 20 years, she would have had no trouble finding another position in her field at a comparable compensation package. The coach and Sandy needed to discover why she continued to stay at the company and what this situation was doing to her that filled her with self-doubt.

The strategy was to start at a basic skills and competency level to determine if the new role was one she could enjoy and in which she was likely to succeed. It was also important to look at the reality of the situation—whether she was actually failing or just feeling that way because of how she was being treated by her boss. Perspective on Sandy's situation would come from exploring such areas as how she managed her boss, whether she could apply past success strategies in these circumstances, and what her boss would say about her performance if he was honest.

Coaching Conversation
The First Meeting

The first coaching conversation with Sandy took place in her office. Initially, she seemed embarrassed and uncomfortable with "exposing" herself to a stranger; in fact, she had been less than enthusiastic about having to "bare her soul" to a complete stranger. Because she was meeting with the coach at the recommendation of her HR department, she came into the meeting with a certain amount of bravado. Her professional wall was up.

She spent a lot of time talking about her past successes and how hard she had worked. She said that her home situation was "handled." She was very candid about the challenges of her position and about her fears. She had made a number of well-thought-out changes in her new role, but it seemed that her boss always found fault and never gave her credit for success.

She talked about the sales department she had inherited and of the challenges and what she had done so far to address them. Sandy felt she had inherited a complacent group of sales managers and a sales staff that was not well trained. She had spent a lot of time in the field talking to customers, which had confirmed her initial feelings. Sandy had instituted a formal sales training program that had been well-received by the salespeople and seemed to elevate their level of knowledge and production.

She had also slowly been trying to replace the dead wood on her management team. She instituted a new pay-for-performance commission plan to reward behaviors that resulted in meeting budgets rather than rewarding seniority, which resulted in some not unwelcome turnover. But despite all her efforts, she continued to get feedback from her boss that she was not doing enough; in fact, her most recent review had been the worst she had ever gotten at the company.

When she talked with her coach about how many hours she worked, she admitted that she was probably too hands-on and that she spent a lot of time chasing after reports that weren't in on time. She felt that she needed to control things tightly because she kept getting second-guessed by her boss. She felt that if she delegated, it would just be one more thing to worry about.

She said being a good mom, providing for her family, and succeeding at whatever she did were most important to her. When her coach asked if she was playing a game she could win, she started crying.

Continuing Coaching Conversations

The coaching continued for the next eight months by telephone. Sandy had to discover who she was again. She had gotten to a point where her children were grateful for any time she had for them, and she defined success by her job rather than who she was as a person and mother or wife. She felt that since she was the main breadwinner, she should just suck it up and get better at pleasing her boss.

The coach forced Sandy to step back and talk through the work decisions she had made and helped her realize they were all solid and producing results. Revenues and morale among the sales force was up, yet she felt that nothing she did was worthwhile. The lack of positive feedback from her boss was crippling her, but she was determined to hang in there until she won the game. The coach offered her a different view of her situation.

The shift in perspective for her was from "proving something" to "honoring her self." As the coach reflected back what she had said and all she had accomplished, Sandy realized that perhaps the problem was not with her, but with her boss. The coach asked a number of questions: Was it possible that her boss resented the changes to "his" team, that anything she changed might be interpreted as an indictment of the way he did it? Was this really about her performance? Upon reflection, she realized that her boss's lack of endorsement probably didn't have anything to do with her performance, rather it was a reflection of his own bruised ego. By hanging on to her need to "prove something," she was destroying her own sense of self-worth and purpose.

Sandy understood that this situation needed to be about who she was and what she did. The other issues were not hers, specifically the difficulties her boss was having in relinquishing control and ownership of his team. If she made changes to the personnel or team structure, he might feel it reflected poorly on him. But was that something she could affect? Sandy realized the challenge was being clear on her values and needs, as well as managing the expectations of her boss. After all, if she changed nothing, she would be out of alignment with what she knew needed to be done. This was an important moment of truth: Was this a game she could win?

The coach asked her to think about what kind of game she felt she could win. She was starting to see positive momentum from her team and she felt they were well on their way to meeting future revenue projections. There were more changes she needed to make for that to happen, but she could envision what was possible and she was focused on the goal she was hired to deliver again. Her energy was back; she was creating her own game. The coach shifted the conversation to one of managing expectations, for her boss and for herself. Sandy redefined the boundaries and rules of the game, and changed her strategy in dealing with her boss so that he was more of a partner than a boss. She had to let go of her ego somewhat, so he could feel a part of the direction in which the company was going. The coach helped her see that she would be better served by including her boss in her thinking on big decisions so he had some ownership in them. It didn't take away any of her autonomy or leadership, but eliminated any lack of support from him once the decision was made. This was a different strategy to help her win her game. Now it was just a matter of execution.

During the time the coach and Sandy were working through the challenges to her career, the toll on her personal life of the travel and the extra hours she was putting in was evident. When the coach asked about self-care, Sandy responded that what little time she had, she tried to spend with her family. Eating right, exercising, and quiet time were all distant memories, losses that she felt were just part of the trade-offs that come with a high-profile, high-pressure job.

When the coach asked what she thought her family wanted from her, she said to be with them more. In fact, her youngest had voiced just that the previous weekend. So at the same time she was designing a new work game, she also started making some changes at home, creating a home game she felt good about. She committed to her children that she would be home by 6:30 each night she wasn't traveling and would not work more than a half day on weekends. The ways to accomplish this came quickly to her once she knew that she had to deliver on her promise to her family. She started delegating more and holding her staff to higher levels of accountability so that she could honor that commitment. She started an exercise program as a first step in a self-care program and asked her children to help support her with it.

Finally, the coach posed the big question: Would this position ever give her the sense of accomplishment and acknowledgment she needed? She decided that she needed to be in an environment that was more encouraging and supportive, but she wasn't ready to let go yet. The final piece needed to be in place before she would leave: She needed to feel that she had done a good job, that she had accomplished everything she had set out to do when she was first promoted and maybe even a little bit more. To that end, she set some goals for herself that would define success by her standards and set a timetable for when that should happen. Surprisingly, this final piece allowed her to breathe. Her personal need for achievement finally helped her find a way to reach closure and win in her current role.

At the same time, she started taking the first steps to explore other opportunities. This was important. She got involved in local industry groups and started networking again. She began reconnecting with the headhunters with whom she hadn't had time to talk earlier. Her total immersion in her job hadn't allowed for time to keep up with colleagues and other rich contact sources. She started using lunch hours as a time to reconnect with people, rather than as a five-minute break at her desk. It was going to take some time to rebuild that network, as well as to put closure on her current role, so Sandy gave herself eight months to deliver her budget and to find a new position. Her relief at setting the date and having an escape plan was huge. Finally she saw a light at the end of the tunnel, and she could get there on her own terms.

Measuring Success

Sandy's initial goal for coaching was to find a way to make her boss acknowledge and support her work, but once she got outside the situation and looked at it through different eyes, she realized her goal was not realistic. She could not change his behavior.

What surfaced as the real goal was for her to get to a point at which she felt good about her work performance and her life outside work. So, the question was how to do that when she had been dependent on the approval of others. Since it was obvious she couldn't win her boss's game, she needed to play a game she could win. Creating her own game forced her to create her own blueprint for success. Where did she want to take the sales force? What revenue goals and accomplishments would reflect success? A succession plan was needed; she had to have the right people and the right structure in place. And what would success look like on a personal level?

Sandy got the picture immediately. She was quickly able to set some revenue goals and a timetable that she felt were ambitious but doable. She made a list of personnel changes to strengthen the organization and set about implementing that plan. She began delegating so she could focus on strategic elements, rather than adding to an already excessively long workweek. She used the feedback from the sales team and customers to measure her effectiveness, as well as measuring performance against the more tangible goals she had developed. Her new game was challenging, but it would provide an end point that would mark success.

These new actions benefited the organization as a whole. Sandy's renewed self-confidence had a positive impact on her sales force.

Because they liked her and respected what she had done so far, they were more than willing to follow her anywhere. They were excited by her new energy and self-confidence and, during a period of economic downturns, they rallied. The removal of poor performers, the additional training programs, and the new esprit d'corps reenergized the team and they felt capable and proud. Sandy worked with them on a strategy they all felt was a stretch, but possible. And they didn't disappoint, delivering revenue well above expectations.

On the homefront, success would be measured by more quality time with the children. Their warm welcome on her arrival each night and her involvement in their basketball games on the weekends made a big difference to both the children and Sandy, not to mention to her husband. He started planning getaways for the two of them one weekend a month, and Sandy finally relaxed enough to let go of work when she was home and enjoy what was important to her.

Today Sandy is six months from achieving the goals she set for herself at work. Although her boss is no more supportive than before, she is not dependent on him to define her success. In six months, she will have accomplished what she set out to accomplish and can feel good about leaving.

In the meantime, she has made a conscious decision to increase her visibility by networking more and getting involved in industry functions. She is aware that she needs to build a pipeline of opportunities so she is controlling her next career move, instead of having it controlled for her. The coach is helping her examine career options and trying to clarify the type of work, surroundings, challenges, and people that will be critical to her personal success and happiness in her next position. Although Sandy is still driven, her life is more balanced, and it is a life in which she feels that she is in control. She is defining what makes her a successful person, not letting others do it for her.

On the personal side, she has found her family be a wonderful source of encouragement, acknowledgement, and good energy. They are pleased to have her back, and this is reflected in her voice and attitude.

Her company also benefited from the money they spent for the coach: Sandy was responsible for delivering a significant addition to the bottom line. An unhappy, distracted, insecure manager is not going to have the confidence and presence to lead a sales team to achieve extraordinary goals. When Sandy got her groove back, the company reaped the dividends, in terms of a motivated staff and improved bottom line.

Lessons Learned

- *The coach must stay detached.* It is easy to get caught up in empathizing with someone who is obviously talented and motivated and who is not recognized for his or her accomplishments. It is critical that coaches detach themselves from their emotions and look at the situation with a fresh eye. By doing that, Sandy's coach was able to take her to a place where she could dispassionately see that part of what was frustrating her was not something that she could affect. At the same time, she could see clearly what it was possible to change.
- *Motivated, driven people need to be able to win.* Sandy was like a hamster on a wheel: She was working harder and faster but not getting the results she wanted. In fact, she was getting results; she was just playing the wrong game. The coach must help the client regain control by creating his or her own game and using that to measure success.
- *Coach the whole person.* If something is upsetting in one part of the client's life, it is probably affecting him or her somewhere else. Ask the questions to get the client in action there as well.
- *The client always has the answer.* She or he may just be asking the wrong question. The coach was able to get Sandy to see that her initial goal was not something she could achieve. Once the focus shifted to looking at the options Sandy had, the flow of ideas and possible solutions came fast.

Questions for Discussion

1. How can the coach detach from empathizing too much with the client?
2. What could have happened if the coaching focused only on Sandy's work situation?
3. How do you get clients to detach from their emotions and to look at their situations through a different set of lenses?
4. What were Sandy's values? Which was most important?
5. How do you shift someone from "doing" to "accomplishment"?

The Author

Kathy Baske Young is a professional certified coach who works with executives and work teams as their partner in both creating and successfully implementing truly extraordinary solutions. She is an International Coach Federation-certified coach and has been coaching full-time since 1999. She is an associate of The Pyramid Resource Group, a corporate coaching company in Cary, North Carolina.

She comes to coaching with 25 years in television sales and sales management experience, most recently as vice president of sales for

WRC-TV, the NBC-owned station in Washington, D.C. Young has coached *Fortune* 500 executives and teams in many fields, including pharmaceuticals, high-tech, telecommunications, broadcasting, finance, real estate investments, and sports.

Young focuses on developing strategic alliances with her partners, and looks to work with clients who are successful, smart, willing to try new ideas, and who have a sense of humor. She and her husband and black lab puppy, Emma, live in the Blue Ridge mountains in Roanoke, Virginia. She can be reached at baskeyoung@mindspring.com.

Coaching the CEO
of a Nonprofit Organization

Metropolitan Nonprofit

Russell Long

The CEO and board chairman of a high-profile nonprofit organization were in a power struggle. An audit had shown that the performance of this metropolitan division was below the average of similar divisions across the country. The board determined that the CEO was not demonstrating the leadership skills to get the organization back on track. The board's executive committee sought consulting and coaching to boost the CEO's performance and turn the division around. The CEO's 360-degree performance review, which was tied to organizational goals, served as the key metric for this coaching relationship.

Organizational Profile

Metropolitan Nonprofit was a division of a nationally respected nonprofit organization that played a prominent role in a growing metropolis of 1.1 million people. With loyal support from the community, the local division had a long list of philanthropic successes that contributed to its favorable image. The staff of approximately 40 worked with a budget exceeding $3 million. The board of directors attracted 25 members of the community and grew to almost 40 during the 15-month coaching contract.

Background

Sam saw his power as CEO slipping. In recent meetings, the chairman had been openly critical of Sam's ability to lead the highly visible

This case was prepared to serve as a basis for discussion rather than to illustrate either effective or ineffective administrative and management practices. Names of places, organizations, or people have been disguised at the request of the author or organization.

organization. As evidence, the chairman cited a recent audit indicating that the organization was performing below average under Sam's leadership. In addition, several projects under his supervision had failed to meet expectations. Sam's 40-member staff suffered from lack of direction and poor communication. New priorities, improved communication, and better relations would be required to get the organization back on track.

The board chairman did not see eye-to-eye with the CEO. Sam resented the board chairman's micromanagement. Their strained relationship affected the morale of the organization's 40 employees, who were losing confidence in Sam's ability to lead. Overall, organizational performance had slipped below the levels of other similar metropolitan divisions. The board determined that performance interventions were required to realize the potential of the organization.

The executive committee searched for management consulting and coaching assistance to address the organizational shortfalls. A coaching relationship was established to provide Sam with personalized assistance to make the necessary changes. The 14-month contract, signed by the executive committee, called for executive coaching for both the chairman and the CEO, as well as strategic planning and board development consulting. The coaching brought about significant improvements in Sam's image, work habits, and relationships. Ultimately, he noted that coaching directly contributed to his job security, improved relations with the board, and increased his own involvement in his rapidly growing city.

Organizational Assessment

The consultant/executive coach scheduled personal interviews with the members of the executive committee and executive staff, as well as key community leaders, to hear their concerns, suggestions for improvement, and other comments. The rest of the staff participated in focus groups on similar topics. Board members and staff members cited the following examples of the strained relationship between the chairman and CEO:

- "The chairman thinks the staff works directly for him."
- "The CEO does not stand up to the chairman and loses credibility."
- "The chairman micromanages staff and does not trust the CEO."
- "The CEO is not being held accountable."

This personality clash was perceived as a roadblock to improved organizational performance. Deteriorating trust in Sam's ability to turn the organization around was affecting staff productivity and morale. This case study will focus on the process and outcomes of Sam's coaching.

The Executive

Sam was 50 years old, with 30 years of experience in nonprofit organizations and three years as CEO at Metropolitan Nonprofit. Since his hiring, the board had changed from an operation and volunteer-focused group to a much larger and more powerful group of business executives. These new board members had different expectations for the organization's performance and growth, and its trust in Sam had eroded due to his lack of focus on results and metric-based reporting. The board was looking for more attention to detail and a clear strategic direction for turning around the organization's performance.

Strategy

Sam agreed to work with his coach to improve his leadership effectiveness and interpersonal dynamics with the chairman. He recognized that his pending performance review for the previous year, along with future reviews, were key measures of organizational and personal success. He also saw the strategic plan as driving the metrics of future success and believed that his coach could provide executive experience and guidance on his performance development.

The coach viewed this coaching relationship as a collaborative effort between himself and the client, supporting the coach's concept that performance business coaching is a partnership that helps clients identify and perform fulfilling results in their work and personal lives. Through coaching, clients deepen their learning, improve their performance, and enhance their quality of life.

In his consulting role, the coach participated in various board meetings, committee meetings, and ongoing interventions to provide management development strategy. The coach shared his real-time observations with Sam and discussed the CEO's impact on organizational effectiveness. Sam found these shadow coaching opportunities valuable in increasing his awareness of his impact in group settings. The Myers-Briggs Type Indicator was used to give the CEO and the chairman more insight into their personalities and preferences and a greater appreciation for their differences.

To facilitate interaction, Sam and the chairman were given a four-quadrant communications style instrument (similar to DISC) that identified their preferred styles of communicating. The coach facilitated several focused coaching sessions in which the CEO and chairman discussed their communication styles and identified ways to better communicate and work together. For example, Sam tended to communicate vision and new initiatives, but the chairman expected a focus on operations and details. Specific agreements were identified to improve communication and ensure understanding on significant issues.

Coaching Conversations
Starting Point

The coaching sessions began with a face-to-face meeting. This onsite kickoff provided a way to share the immediate environment of the person being coached, to discuss confidentiality, and to co-design the relationship. Subsequent coaching occurred over the phone, with the exception of such shadow coaching sessions as observations in meetings, presentations, and reporting.

Access Point

Sam casually mentioned a concern that he might be seen as somewhat "aloof" by some of his staff. His coach asked him to consider if this might be true, based on the physical barriers of his office, but by the next coaching session Sam had not discovered any ways his office setting might create an obstacle with his staff. The coach requested that the CEO visually walk through the office building from the perspective of a visitor or new employee and describe what he saw. This required him to see his familiar surroundings in a new way. As the coach had observed, Sam's office was isolated, "guarded" by several assistants facing the entrance, and furnished with an enormous executive desk. Sam acknowledged that his work area was somewhat distant, exclusive, and different from others. As a result of this revelation, Sam created a plan to communicate more often and more openly with his staff. He began to circulate around the building for more impromptu conversations and to plan for a new building with more equitable office space for his staff.

Point of Action

Shortly after the coaching sessions began, Sam received a "provisional" performance review for the previous year. He received a subsequent six-month review that was also "provisional." He then had only four months before his annual review. Unless a change occurred, Sam would be terminated. During a coaching session in the boardroom, the coach asked Sam to stand behind the chair the chairman occupied during board meetings and to articulate the key outcomes that were expected of him. He was then asked to move to another seat at the table and state the things that he liked to do, and always did, by default. When he was asked what the outcome would be if he continued to do things by default, Sam admitted that he might be terminated. His coach asked, "Which set of expectations and outcomes will you commit to?" Sam recognized with new clarity the difference between what he liked to do and what he needed to do. He committed to do what the board was asking of him. He asked the coach to hold him accountable for this commitment.

Point of Celebration

When Sam received his annual 360-degree evaluation, he was happy that the leadership recognized his contribution with a "commendable" review. He saw that the changes he had made were working and that his performance review clearly communicated his accomplishments. He was quite pleased to have a much better working relationship with the new chairman of the board.

He celebrated his success with an informal external CEO support group he had helped to establish some six months earlier and with his friends and family. He thanked his staff for their hard work. He also celebrated the work he did in his coaching. When asked about a key shift in perspective that had occurred for him, Sam stated that he had come to see the chairman as a stepping stone rather than a stumbling block to his success. He took steps to understand his new chairman and to cocreate their relationship. Sam was acknowledged for his openness to exploring and implementing new behaviors and valuing new approaches to old issues.

Measuring Success

Six months after the conclusion of coaching, Sam stated that he had become more aware of his strengths and weaknesses, impact on others, personality, and communication style. The coaching sessions also showed him how to be more open with relationships and celebrate successes. He gave his coaching an 88 out of 100 satisfaction points. Among other successes, the CEO noted that coaching directly contributed to his improved relations with both the board and staff, and his increased involvement in his rapidly growing city. The coach's reference articles, fieldwork between sessions, and challenging questions prompted him to seek his own answers through new ways of problem solving and thinking.

Sam realized that before coaching he had done what he found enjoyable and would often delay other essential work. His procrastination eventually hurt his credibility. "Today, I tackle the work I don't enjoy first so I am motivated to get to the work I prefer." He said he is more comfortable being who he is with the adjustments he made during coaching.

Sam highlighted the annual 360-degree performance review, with its jointly determined outcome measures, as a key measure of success. He now plays a role in the establishment of his key outcomes, which eliminates misunderstandings and creates a common commitment to future action with the board leadership. He has a much-improved relationship with the executive committee due to his continuing efforts to meet with them individually outside of official meetings.

Sam acknowledges that the return-on-investment for his coaching is beyond calculation. He stated that when coaching began, he was a candidate for an unfair termination due to the relationship with the chairman. He said this would have caused significant personal and organizational damage, with potential lawsuits and adverse media coverage. Instead, this relationship was significantly improved, his work focus was changed, and he had improved his management style. He is now proud that he and the board share the same vision and strategic plan, which they jointly developed.

When asked about the intangible benefits of coaching he said, "I feel better about who I am and how I do my job. I have less stress and I share successes with others. I now fully enjoy my work." In addition, Sam learned to explore new ways of performing. "I better understand myself, my values, and my working relationships. Consequently, I now look beyond my normal patterns for new solutions and possibilities."

Lessons Learned

- *Ask powerful questions.* Effective coaches ask powerful questions that lead to client-determined learning and action.
- *Push for accountability.* When the client responds with easy answers or does not honor commitments, "push back" to encourage reflection and accountability.
- *Clients may be hesitant to open up to a coach.* The CEO had a cautious and reserved demeanor, which prevented him from speaking openly about his feelings, perceptions, and fears. An initial focus on task accomplishment created a safe place to build trust before shifting to more personal issues.

- *Honesty is still the best policy.* Before coaching, Sam did not have candid relationships with his staff or board members and was unaware of the specific faults that contributed to his unfavorable image. Clients must be willing to tell the truth, even if it's painful.
- *Trust intuition.* Trust and articulate coaching intuition to increase truth telling, speed up action, and see through blind spots to changed behavior.
- *Experience counts.* Draw on your prior business experience and coaching knowledge to assist the client. Introduce new perspectives to problems. Guide the client through complex situations to discover his or her best solution.
- *Seek satisfaction.* Coaching was initially provided to Sam and the chairman at the same time to ensure a depth of assistance, but Sam eventually wanted to work one-on-one. Coaching must work for both parties involved.
- *Confidentiality and mutual respect are essential.* Confidentiality and mutual respect in the coaching relationship will help the client see through blind spots and change behaviors.
- *Recognize achievements.* The importance of genuine acknowledgement for the small yet important achievements is also significant in reinforcing changed actions.
- *Believe.* Believing at times in the CEO's capabilities more than he himself believed in them was significant in fostering change.
- *Coaching and consulting can be done together with the client.* The coach was also the consultant here. Establishing clear boundaries around each role was necessary and worked. The client needs to understand these boundaries.

Questions for Discussion
1. What precipitated the need for coaching in this case?
2. Who saw the need for coaching here?
3. What breakthroughs did Sam achieve from his coaching?
4. What insight did Sam attain of himself?
5. What would the result most likely have been without coaching?

The Author
Russell Long holds master's degrees in business administration and health-care administration. He is the president of Change Innovations, a management consulting, training, and executive coaching firm, and vice president of Corporate Coach U, an accredited

international business coach training and service organization. Long's clients include executives and professionals in *Fortune* 500, nonprofit, and government organizations, as well as entrepreneurs. Long is chairman of the membership committee of the International Coaching Federation (ICF) in Washington, D.C., and founding officer of his metropolitan ICF chapter. He can be reached at rlong@changeinnovations.com or www.changeinnovations.com.

Coaching Builds Strong Foundation for a Start-Up Health-Care Clinic

Marcia Reynolds

The client, the general manager of a start-up health-care clinic, hired a coach to be her silent partner. This was the client's first experience in starting a business and in reporting to an all-male corporate management team in another state. She looked to her coach for guidance in negotiating with superiors, vendors, and staff to develop a strong team of employees and to keep perspective in her private life. In the six-month process, the client developed a strong relationship with her superiors and peers, created a fully operational health-care clinic, and carved out time to maintain her family and her health.

Organizational Profile

Wendy, a 39-year-old general manager of a new women's health-care clinic in Phoenix, Arizona, hired an executive coach during her first week in the position. The clinic was one of a chain headquartered in California. As the general manager of the first clinic in Arizona, Wendy also represented the Arizona branch of the corporation. The vision was to open five clinics in the state within five years.

Wendy reported to the president of the corporation, but her performance and decisions were also subject to the scrutiny of the medical director.

Background

Wendy hired a coach because she saw her new position as an opportunity to build on her professional credibility with a start-up

This case was prepared to serve as a basis for discussion rather than to illustrate either effective or ineffective administrative and management practices. Names of places, organizations, or people have been disguised at the request of the author or organization.

success story. Her goal was to demonstrate that in one year she could take an organization from inception to fully functional—operating with a high-performing team of employees, a patient waiting list for highly coveted appointments, and a positive, visible presence in the community. This clinic would then be the model for four more planned for the Phoenix area. In addition, Wendy had a six-year-old child at home. She wanted to remain an active parent while maintaining some sense of balance and good health for herself.

Before starting, Wendy identified three particular management skills to focus on in the process of coaching:

- *delegation:* communicating expectations and holding people accountable for performance
- *communicating up:* setting boundaries and making difficult requests of the top corporate executives, specifically the president, medical director, and marketing director
- *negotiations:* successful bargaining with outside vendors, clinical and sales staff, and members of the corporate management team.

Because the first challenges she faced were to rent office space and to hire the team to run the clinic, the coaching would also cover the step-by-step procedures for starting a new business.

Strategy

In accordance with the definition of coaching laid out by the International Coach Federation, the coaching relationship in this situation was designed to help the client reach a higher level of performance, learning, and satisfaction than she could have achieved without a coach. The coach would help Wendy reach this point through dialogue, inquiry, and making requests to promote action toward her desired outcomes. Advice, opinions, and suggestions were occasionally offered, based on the coach's experience in teaching management communications and life management skills. However, this advice was made only when Wendy requested it and with the understanding that the client was free to accept or decline what was offered. During the initial session, Wendy agreed to take ultimate responsibility for her actions.

The coach and Wendy agreed to meet for 30-minute weekly sessions since so many critical decisions and interactions were necessary during the start-up process. Because Wendy would be traveling frequently to California, and even when home didn't feel as if she had total control of her schedule, they agreed that meeting by phone would be most convenient. Wendy agreed to honor all time commitments made with her coach.

To make the most of the time spent in each session, the client agreed to fill out a Coaching Prep Form prior to making the call to focus on the key issues she wanted to resolve in each session. The prep form asked her to define the actions taken since the previous call, the obstacles that hindered her progress, and the goals she would like to achieve during that coaching session.

After the second session exceeded the 30-minute timeframe, the coach and Wendy agreed to determine at the beginning of the calls how much time would be given to each of the three major areas: communication with the executive team; operation of the clinic, including her relationship to employees; and family and self-care. This served to force Wendy to assess her progress and roadblocks in all three areas as well as to balance the time she spent on each area. After one month of this practice, the coach and Wendy found that the 30-minute sessions were more efficient. They no longer had a time problem; in fact, they accomplished more in less time.

The Coaching Conversation

Prior to the first meeting, Wendy was given a Personal Profile Assessment to determine her dominant interactive style and a Values Inventory to identify the lens through which she appraised the world and the people around her. Both assessments provided information throughout the coaching relationship on how Wendy could best adapt her style for results when interacting with others.

The first session was held in person. Subsequent sessions were held on the phone every week for three months. At three months, Wendy and her coach held a second face-to-face session to review progress and goals, and the relationship continued by phone for a second three-month cycle.

Starting Point

The initial conversation was used to identify strengths and weaknesses of Wendy's leadership style and points of focus for the coaching sessions. Drawing on the results of the Personal Profile Assessment and Values Inventory, the coach and client agreed that Wendy's greatest strengths were her abilities to build one-on-one rapport with her employees, identify the priorities of tasks to be completed, and build positive relationships with the media and the community.

Points of Focus

Wendy's points of focus centered on her difficulties in clearly stating her expectations and performance measures when delegating, confronting problems both with her own superiors and with her staff, and maintaining a healthy and happy personal life outside work.

Access Points

Wendy made several significant discoveries during the time she worked with her coach. These discoveries were the following:

- *Although she had great needs for respect, feeling worthwhile, and being heard, so did her superiors.* Therefore, feeding the ego needs of the president and the medical director by sincerely praising them, acknowledging their work, and building on their ideas instead of resisting them served her well in the long run. She had felt a growing tension between herself and the two men, but the change in their behavior toward her over time reflected not only a decrease in their defensiveness but also an increased likelihood that they would honor her requests. In a short time after making these adjustments to her style, she found that disagreeing with their ideas and making requests for items that stretched the budget met with little resistance. She might not get what she asked for, but the discussions were professional and considerate. "Confrontation" became easy when she was viewed as an ally instead of an agitator.
- *Delegation is easier when everyone is operating with the same vision.* Once her team had been hired, Wendy held a visioning session during which the employees created the picture of what the clinic would look like at its best in one year. Then they designed their own job descriptions and negotiated priorities together. Wendy found that since she wasn't a "detail person" who gave good directions and clear expectations, she could compensate by having the team help her create the plan and performance measures. As a result, her employees reported feeling like they were a family, which increased performance and decreased conflict.
- *"I'll do it when . . ." means "I'll never get around to it."* Wendy kept putting off her self-care as something she would do after the clinic was running smoothly. Once she explored the phrase "running smoothly," she realized that this could take much longer—maybe forever—to achieve. "Running smoothly" could in fact conflict with "success" if the picture of success included managing a growing business in which change is a constant. She had to stay healthy to be the vital and agile conductor of this orchestra. So she began walking regu-

larly, promised to quit taking business home with her on the weekends so she could give 100 percent to her family, and rejoined the church choir. As a result, she reported an improvement in her decision-making and creative abilities at work.

Point of Action

During the six-month coaching period, Wendy rented space and opened the clinic, hired and trained a team of employees, established a respectful relationship with her superiors, and incorporated family time and self-care into her busy schedule. Facing obstacles at every turn, she felt that by working with her coach she had created her start-up success story.

Point of Celebration

The insight Wendy shared when she and her coach met for lunch in her last coaching session focused on her perspective. She felt that she had spent six months engrossed in the tactical operations of the clinic; her role had been steeped in managing. She now felt that she could step back and spend more time on the strategic point of view, for both the growth of the current clinic and the future openings of other clinics in Phoenix. She could now take on some aspects of leadership. The coach called the lunch a graduation, after which Wendy could make the transition from the role of manager to the role of leader.

Measuring Success

Because Wendy had hired the coach on her own, she did not engage in any formal measurement of the results. However, she completed a progress report that included her satisfaction with the process and her perspective on the effect coaching had on her success. In particular, she stated that she had met the goals she had cited at the beginning of the process, including an increase in her delegation and communication skills, and that she felt the coaching had broadened her executive competencies beyond skill development. The results had exceeded her expectations. In particular, she had gained new strategies for developing relationships with employees and management. She felt more confident in her role as an executive, and no longer felt as if being a woman was a detriment to her career; in fact, she found strength in her gender and her style. She acknowledged the distinction between manager and leader as a difference in role, not capability. This allowed her to step into her role as manager with clarity and strength of purpose. She had also found that she could lead a full and happy life by setting priorities and staying focused in the moment. Although there would always be difficulties and unexpected problems, she felt more in control.

Lessons Learned

Wendy and her coach created a new definition of the word "leader." In an early conversation, they discussed how she could be a leader through her actions instead of a manager, as if being a manager was bad. It quickly became apparent that, in her start-up capacity, Wendy's primary responsibilities, accountabilities, and outcomes required her to be a manager. Her focus was tactical, at least during the first six months. She had to make more decisions than delegate, she had to set her sights more on the moment than the big picture, and she had to make many decisions on her own instead of including everyone in the process (especially since all her hires were new). All of this gave legitimacy to her title of general manager and permission to take control and wield her authority. Wendy then created a vision of what the organization would look like when it was time to make the transition to a more strategic leadership role. The victory celebration at the end of six months included her graduation from powerful manager to wise leader.

Questions for Discussion

1. According to roles and responsibilities, when does a manager make the transition to leader?
2. What roles define both a manager and a leader? Does a manager always have to aspire to be a leader?
3. What factors should be considered when learning to successfully "manage up"?
4. What work circumstances, if any, might preclude someone from maintaining a self-care regimen?
5. How do the skills of endorsing and praising fit into the art of negotiating?

The Author

Marcia Reynolds is a master certified coach and past president of the International Coach Federation. She holds two master's degrees, one of which is in educational technology. Reynolds works with individuals and organizations to help them become more emotionally intelligent and create successful working environments. She works internationally, coaching executives and professionals, and presenting keynote speeches and training in Taiwan, Thailand, Australia, and England, as well as across the United States and Canada. Her clients include Medtronic, Bank One, Kaiser Permanente, DOW Chemical, the U.S. Department of Health and Human Services, and the National Institutes of Health. Excerpts from her books, tapes, and interviews have appeared in *Fortune* and *Health* magazines, *Investor's Business Daily,* and *The New York Times,* and she has appeared on ABC World News, National Public Radio, and Japan Nightly News. She can be reached at phone: 602.954.9030; email: Marcia@covisioning.com; or www.OutsmartYourBrain.com.

A Billing Organization Discovers New Ways of Doing Business

Vision Telecom

Ellen Fredericks and Laura Berman Fortgang

This story showcases the impact of an individual and team coaching initiative for a billing operations organization within the telecommunications industry. The purpose of the coaching engagement was to assist an executive in gaining clarity about the future vision for his information technology and billing organization of more than 300 people and to align the organization in the new direction.

The new organization strategy was developed and adopted within six months as the billing operations started to shift from a cost center to a customer- and value-focused organization.

Background

Vision Telecom is a global provider of telecommunications services, serving both business and consumer markets with offices around the world. Mark was the executive responsible for leading the billing and industry relations organization of more than 300 information technology and billing managers within the network and computing services division. Historically this division had operated as a cost center providing services to other divisions within the company. In addition, the majority of employees were Vision Telecom managers, with a small percentage of work being outsourced or contracted to other companies.

Because he had spent most of his career in sales and marketing, this was a new role for Mark. He recognized that due to the intense

This case was prepared to serve as a basis for discussion rather than to illustrate either effective or ineffective administrative and management practices. Names of places, organizations, or people have been disguised at the request of the author or organization.

competition in the industry the organization needed to do business differently but wasn't clear on exactly how. He considered hiring a coach to help him make the transition to the new position while gaining clarity about the future direction and vision for the organization. His newly formed leadership team wasn't yet working well together, and he was also challenged by the analytical style of his highly technical staff. His decision to actually hire a coach occurred while having lunch with a former colleague turned executive coach, who proposed a coaching strategy.

Mark and the coach identified a number of goals for the coaching:

- increasing the executive's ability to communicate easily with technical staff
- creating a high performing leadership team
- shifting the executive's strategic focus from 10 percent of his time to at least 30 percent
- holding the division's managers accountable for their commitments and results
- resolving real and perceived obstacles quickly.

Strategy

The coaching in this engagement focused on creating awareness on the part of Mark and his direct reports, designing actions that led to agreed upon results, and managing progress and accountability. The engagement included

- one year of individual coaching for the executive (in person and telephone)
- a two-day group coaching session to be held two to three months into the coaching
- six months of in-person group coaching for the leadership team of 15 managers.

The fee structure was to be as follows:

- a retainer for three months of in-person coaching for Mark
- a two-day project fee for the leadership group coaching
- a retainer for nine months of coaching, to include individual in-person and telephone coaching for the executive and in-person group coaching for the leadership team.

The Executive Coaching

Mark's coaching for the first three months was designed to meet the needs identified by the coach in the initial consultation, which are illustrated in table 1.

Table 1. Identification of needs.

Need/Skill	Coaching Objective
Leadership	Expand leadership styles to include coaching and democratic styles
	Define characteristics of a high-performing team
	Create team standards and systems of accountability
Strategic thinking	Create a shared vision, purpose, and values
Communication	Increase ease and comfort working with technical associates
Time management	Increase strategic thinking and planning time to 30 percent per month

Each coaching session focused on one or more of these areas through inquiry and tools designed to move the client forward. Table 2 was used during the first month of coaching to support Mark in creating a shared vision, purpose, and values for the organization.

To ensure the highest probability for success, Mark was requested
- to honor his individual and group coaching appointments
- to encourage and expect his leadership team to do the same
- to model the tools and techniques learned in coaching
- to set monthly goals with the leadership team and monitor progress.

Group Coaching

A two-day group coaching session with the leadership team took place at the end of three months. The purpose was to align the team on shared vision, purpose, and values, using Mark's vision as a foundation for discussion. To encourage innovation and initiative in creating greater customer value, each member of the team designed breakthrough projects. A breakthrough project was defined as a project that would
- positively affect customer value or profit by at least 25 percent
- not have been undertaken in a "business as usual" environment due to its perceived risks
- be approved by 80 percent of the team members.

The monthly group coaching that began the following month was designed to help the leadership team to do the following:
- create and implement a plan to cascade the vision and values throughout the entire organization

Table 2. Vision, purpose, and values of coaching.

VISION A picture of our desired future	PURPOSE What the organization exists to do	VALUES How we intend to operate on a daily basis
What are the most influential trends in our industry today? What critical events, inside or outside the company, could take place within the near future that could affect our organization? What are the top five products and/or services that we could produce and deliver? Without access to these products or services, what value will the customer miss? What kind of customers do we want to have?	For what reason do we want this organization to exist? What is the value that we will bring to our customers? To our suppliers? What results do we want to be known for? What contributions do we want to make?	What's most important to us? What reputation will we have? In what ways will people work together that honor what we say is most important?

- remove perceived and real obstacles to successful implementation
- provide shared language and tools to facilitate more effective team communication.

The Coaching Conversation
Starting Point

During the first coaching session, the coach's objective was to keep Mark focused on creating solutions and outcomes rather than on information and details from the past. The coach distinguished an information-seeking approach from a wisdom-seeking approach to solving problems and creating outcomes. This is illustrated in table 3.

Shifting the focus away from information seeking required the coach to find the best questions for drawing out the results that Mark was seeking for his organization. The coach focused this session on four questions to draw out Mark's best thinking and wisdom:

- What do you want to be known for?
- What is working in the organization?
- What would you do differently?
- What would the organization be doing differently if it was 25 percent bolder?

Table 3. Information-seeking versus wisdom-seeking approach.

Characteristics of Information Seeker	Characteristics of Wisdom Seeker
Asks questions that are self-centered	Asks questions that are focused outward
Asks questions that are past-based	Asks questions that are future-focused (Wisdom Access Questions)
Digs for evidence to justify point of view	Explores as an objective observer to find truth
Is oriented toward problems	Is oriented toward solutions
Must have or give answers as part of identity	Comfortable waiting for answers and with appearing to "not know" temporarily

Adapted with permission from *Living Your Best Life*, Laura Fortgang, J.P. Tarcher/Putnam, 2001.

Access Point

The first question helped Mark identify how he personally wanted to be known by senior management, the leadership team and organization, customers, and suppliers. The next two questions clarified that the way the team had done business was no longer meeting the needs of customers, suppliers, and the senior management team. The industry dynamics were changing rapidly, with greater competition, faster time-to-market requirements, and a focus on delivering value to the customer. This was an organization that historically had dictated strategy and plans rather than partnering with customers to identify and meet their needs. The question "what would the organization be doing differently if it was 25 percent bolder" was the access point, at which the executive saw clearly that he wanted to transform the organization to a value-creating (profit and loss) organization rather than to just improve productivity within a cost center. This question was posed because it appeared that Mark's thinking was limited by what he believed was possible within the current management framework.

Point of Action and Celebration

It was evident at the six-month mark that significant progress had been made in aligning the organization with the vision. The vision was regularly mentioned at team meetings, and goals were linked to the big picture. More partnering and planning was being done with key business partners and customers. Within a one-year timeframe, the organization had significantly changed the way it did business and was making decisions for projects and budgets on customer needs, strategic value, and productivity as opposed to merely financial savings. Customers and suppliers viewed the organization as one that was creating value.

Measuring Success

Success was determined by Mark and his coach together and focused primarily on key results Mark saw as critical:

- Mark's clear understanding of vision, purpose, and values (within two months)
- alignment of the leadership team with vision, purpose, and values (within three months)
- adoption of the vision and values across the majority of the organization (within six months)
- decisions for projects made on customer need, strategic value, and productivity improvement rather than just cost savings (within nine months)
- organization viewed as creating value (within one year)
- coaching viewed as positively affecting goals and learning (monthly).

The key measure of success for the coaching engagement was the shortening of the alignment and adoption process beyond the two years Mark initially thought would be needed.

The following needs that had been identified by the coach at the beginning of the engagement and addressed as a result of the coaching were considered to be secondary measures of success:

- increasing Mark's ability to communicate easily with technical staff
- creating a high-performance leadership team
- shifting Mark's strategic focus from 10 percent to at least 30 percent
- holding the managers accountable for their commitments and results
- resolving real and perceived obstacles quickly.

Lessons Learned

Lessons learned from the experiences were the following:

- *Structuring the engagement to allow multiple members of the team to be coached as a group or individually is key for success.* Without the endorsement of the entire leadership team, the vision and values have a lower probability of becoming shared throughout the organization.
- *Obtaining the executive's commitment to the coaching process is a must.* A leader who "walks the talk" brings greater credibility to the initiative. Without it, the coaching impact is greatly reduced.
- *Creating success milestones help the client and organization celebrate success and see the impact of the coaching process along the way.* Interim celebrations help to maintain the organization's momentum.

- *Coach the client to set objectives for the coaching engagement that are specific and measurable.* This will ensure that the value of the coaching is recognized and acknowledged. If the client can't see tangible value as a result of the coaching initiative, he or she will not speak positively to others about the value of coaching.

Questions for Discussion

1. What other approaches to the coaching strategy could have been considered for this engagement?
2. What other criteria could be used to measure success?
3. What is the value of the executive gaining clarity on vision, purpose, and values before working with the leadership team?
4. In what ways might the outcomes have been different if the leadership team had not aligned with the new direction and values?
5. How might individual coaching for the leadership team have accelerated the results?

The Authors

Ellen Fredericks is a coaching partner and the vice president of business development and coaching for LBF InterCoach. She is a master certified coach. Ellen's clients include executives and leaders seeking to take their individual, team, or organizational performance to the next level; build organizational cultures that reflect their vision and values; and develop leaders that can consistently produce new levels of results in the face of rapid change and competition. As a former corporate executive, Ellen brings 25 years of business and management experience to her coaching from the telecommunications industry, where she held diverse positions in marketing, information technology, sales, operations, human resources, and government affairs. She can be reached at InterCoach, Inc., 26 Park St., Suite 2045, Montclair, NJ 07042; phone: 973.857.8180; email: ellen@intercoach.com.

Laura Berman Fortgang, founder and president of LBF InterCoach, is the author of *Living Your Best Life* (Tarcher/Putnam) and *Take Yourself to the Top* (Warner Books). She can be reached at lbf@intercoach.com.

About the Editor

Darelyn "DJ" Mitsch is a master certified coach, one of the first 25 designated by the International Coach Federation (ICF). As the immediate past president of the ICF, Mitsch lead the association across borders to become recognized as the global professional society of coaches.

Mitsch founded the Pyramid Resource Group, The Corporate Coaching Company, in 1994 with her life and business partner Barry Mitsch. The company was innovative in attracting and mentoring a masterful group of coaches who team to serve *Fortune* 500 and international corporations. Her client list includes the world's largest telecommunications companies, pharmaceutical companies, real estate investment firms, high-tech innovators, medical nonprofits, broadcasting companies, and professional sports organizations.

Executive and team coaching are Mitsch's passion. She has worked with over 300 executive clients, managers, and business owners to help them get more out of life than six-figure salaries and prematurely gray hair. The teams Mitsch coaches achieve extraordinary business goals through her trademarked program, The Extraordinary Game. She has written culture changing "coaching" initiatives for in-house organizational development teams to teach coaching skills to managers.

Prior to entering the coaching field, Mitsch had a highly successful 16-year career as a broadcast executive. As a broadcaster, she managed new project startups and was hired as a turnaround specialist. Responsible for operations, sales, administration, finance, marketing, promotions, and facilities construction, she consistently reported to a chairman and board of directors in her executive roles.

Mitsch is known for her big heart, compassion, humor, straight talk, and business savvy. Her personal mission is to "reawaken a sense of purpose in people and challenge teams to become innovative and have more fun!" She is the mother of two wise children, Jessica, 12, and Hank, 8, whom she claims came to the planet to teach her.

Mitsch regularly speaks as a keynote presenter and workshop facilitator on leadership topics. She can be reached at the Pyramid Resource Group, 1919 Evans Rd., Cary, NC 27513; phone: 919.677.9300, ext 101; email: dj@pyramidresource.com.

About the Series Editor

Jack J. Phillips is a world-renowned expert on measurement and evaluation and developer of the ROI process, a revolutionary process that provides bottom-line figures and accountability for all types of training, performance improvement, human resources, and technology programs. He is the author or editor of more than 30 books—12 focused on measurement and evaluation—and more than 100 articles.

His expertise in measurement and evaluation is based on more than 27 years of corporate experience in five industries (aerospace, textiles, metals, construction materials, and banking). Phillips has served as training and development manager at two *Fortune* 500 firms, senior HR officer at two firms, president of a regional federal savings bank, and management professor at a major state university.

In 1992, Phillips founded Performance Resources Organization (PRO), an international consulting firm that provides comprehensive assessment, measurement, and evaluation services for organizations. In 1999, PRO was acquired by the Franklin Covey Company and is now known as The Jack Phillips Center for Research. Today the center is an independent leading provider of measurement and evaluation services to the global business community. Phillips consults with clients in manufacturing, service, and government organizations in the United States, Canada, Sweden, England, Belgium, Germany, Italy, Holland, South Africa, Mexico, Venezuela, Malaysia, Indonesia, Hong Kong, Australia, New Zealand, and Singapore. Phillips leads the center's research and publishing efforts that support the knowledge and development of assessment, measurement, and evaluation.

Books most recently authored by Phillips include *The Human Resources Scorecard: Measuring the Return on Investment*, Butterworth-Heinemann, Boston, MA, 2001; *The Consultant's Scorecard*, McGraw-Hill, New York, NY, 2000; *HRD Trends Worldwide: Shared Solutions to Compete in a Global Economy*, Butterworth-Heinemann, Boston, MA, 1999; *Return on Investment in Training and Performance Improvement Programs*, Butterworth-Heinemann, Boston, MA, 1997; *Handbook of Training Evaluation and Measurement Methods*, 3rd edition, Butterworth-Heinemann,

Boston, MA, 1997; and *Accountability in Human Resource Management,* Butterworth-Heinemann, Boston, MA, 1996.

Phillips has undergraduate degrees in electrical engineering, physics, and mathematics from Southern Polytechnic State University and Oglethorpe University; a master's degree in decision sciences from Georgia State University; and a Ph.D. in human resource management from the University of Alabama. In 1987 he won the Yoder-Heneman Personnel Creative Application Award from the Society for Human Resource Management.

Phillips can be reached at The Jack Phillips Center for Research, P.O. Box 380637, Birmingham, AL 35238-0637; phone: 205.678.8038; fax: 205.678.0177; email: serieseditor@aol.com.

The Value of Belonging

ASTD membership keeps you up to date on the latest developments in your field, and provides top-quality, *practical* information to help you stay ahead of trends, polish your skills, measure your progress, demonstrate your effectiveness, and advance your career.

We give you what you need most from the entire scope of workplace learning and performance:

Information
We're your best resource for research, best practices, and background support materials – the data you need for your projects to excel.

Networking
We're the facilitator who puts you in touch with colleagues, experts, field specialists, and industry leaders – the people you need to know to succeed.

Technology
We're the clearinghouse for new technologies in training, learning, and knowledge management in the workplace – the background you need to stay ahead.

Analysis
We look at cutting-edge practices and programs and give you a balanced view of the latest tools and techniques – the understanding you need on what works and what doesn't.

Competitive Edge
ASTD is your leading resource on the issues and topics that are important to you. That's the value of belonging!

For more information, or to become a member, please call 1.800.628.2783 (U.S.) or +1.703.683.8100; visit our Website at **www.astd.org**; or send an email to customercare@astd.org.

ASTD
Linking People.
Learning & Performance